An Introduction to
Tchaikovsky's Operas

AN INTRODUCTION TO
TCHAIKOVSKY'S OPERAS,

Henry Zajaczkowski, H.

Westport, Connecticut
London

Library of Congress Cataloging-in-Publication Data

Zajaczkowski, Henry, 1955–
   An introduction to Tchaikovsky's operas / Henry Zajaczkowski.
     p. cm.
   Includes bibliographical references and index.
   ISBN 0–275–97949–0 (alk. paper)
     1. Tchaikovsky, Peter Ilich, 1840–1893. Operas. I. Title
   MT100.C4Z34   2005
   782.1'092—dc22   2004028154

British Library Cataloguing in Publication Data is available.

Library of Congress Catalog Card Number: 2004028154
ISBN: 0–275–97949–0

First published in 2005

Praeger Publishers, 88 Post Road West, Westport, CT 06881
An imprint of Greenwood Publishing Group, Inc.
www.praeger.com

Printed in the United States of America

The paper used in this book complies with the
Permanent Paper Standard issued by the National
Information Standards Organization (Z39.48–1984).

10 9 8 7 6 5 4 3 2 1

10/05

In memory of my parents

Part of the composer's sketch of Natalia's arioso in Act 1 of *The Oprichnik*

CONTENTS

PREFACE

Why some of a composer's works become established in the international repertoire while others that are of no less value remain obscure cannot always be rationally explained. Perhaps it is a necessary part of our collective cultural experience, an element of impenetrable mystery far more intangibly life-defining than mere explainability.

In Tchaikovsky's case, his nine extant operas have only yielded two of their number into familiarity: *Eugene Onegin* and *The Queen of Spades*. The remainder, however, are no unworthy efforts, comprising another two, *The Maid of Orléans* and *The Enchantress*, that are to be considered among the Romantic period's greatest operas, and a range of other works spanning unevenness and greatness. Moreover, how can his operas' variable fortunes be reconciled with the almost uncanny acumen displayed in his output of ballets—*Swan Lake, The Sleeping Beauty,* and *The Nutcracker*—which are widely acknowledged to have revivified and enriched nineteenth-century ballet, saving it both in musical and dramatic terms from the stale comfortableness of convention into which it had sunk? As R.J. Wiley put it, Tchaikovsky "took ballet music out of the hands of Minkus and delivered it into the hands of Stravinsky."[1] This is not to suggest that Tchaikovsky wrought similar changes in the field of opera; he was no iconoclast in that regard, steering, rather, a fairly moderate course, with only occasional experimentation in compositional methods, but it is at least fair to say that the innate dramatic sense that guided his pen in the writing of ballets did not desert him when he wrote operas. Stravinsky himself considered Tchaikovsky his nation's greatest opera composer, a view with which Prokofiev somewhat wryly and all the more significantly agreed, noting that it was "maybe not often the case"[2] that he and his great rival (both living in 1930s Paris at the time) shared an opinion.

The two well-known operas each represent a dichotomy in their reception by the public and the critics. The libretti of both were adapted from Pushkin, causing adverse reaction from those pundits who consider the texts of that literary giant too loosely rendered in the transformation; indeed it has often been thought that he was travestied by the process. Operas are, however, frequently only a résumé of their original written source, and the critical focus upon this matter, in the case of those two works, has arguably been excessive. *The Queen of Spades* has perhaps suffered the more severely in this regard (although certainly *Eugene Onegin* has received some severe barbs), for it largely replaces Pushkin's ironical tone with an emphasis upon the gothic, a ghost story instead of a sardonic commentary upon the human condition. Some rehabilitation of this drama is clearly necessary in critical terms, for it is a far more sophisticated work than the critics (but not, it seems, the public) generally allow, and in view of this, more space is allocated to an assessment of it here than to *Onegin*.

The analytical approach in this study is mostly aimed to be suitable for a broad readership, including the nonmusician as well as the musician, with fairly restricted use of technical musical terminology (although there is inevitably a certain quantity of it). I have placed composers' dates after the first occurrence of their names, and have done so, for the sake of consistency, even in respect to the most well known of them. The main purpose of the book is one of description rather than detailed analysis, namely to provide a brief, general overview of Tchaikovsky's operatic output, to demonstrate its range and a little of its depth, and to give an indication, therefore, of why most of it, in an ideal world, should be well-known, rather than unfathomably neglected.

The present text originated in a different format. Following a kind invitation to me from the distinguished biographer and cultural historian Alexander Poznansky to join him as co-author of a general reference book on Tchaikovsky, I began writing a chapter on the composer's operas. My parents passed away during that work, and administrative matters in regard to their estate inevitably meant that less time was available for it. Despite the reconfiguring of the reference book as a symposium, with Poznansky and myself as co-editors, and the appointment of several other specialists to write other chapters, I made no further progress on the opera chapter. Ultimately, having been unable, due to constraints on available time, to connect as fully with editorial matters as I would have wished, I disengaged from the project, with much regret and with a still-unfinished chapter on Tchaikovsky's operas. That chapter, revised and completed, has become the present book.

Regarding procedural points: firstly, transliteration of Russian words and names has been done according to an adaptation of the American Library of Congress system. Complete uniformity in transliteration is, however, always complicated by the fact that some names have come to be rendered traditionally, Tchaikovsky's itself being a prime case, for the initial "T" is in fact spurious. Tchaikovsky has been known for too great a time since his death with his name in that spelling for it to be likely for a different standard transliteration to be accepted, although he will be encountered with "Ch" at the start of his name in many scholarly sources. Other difficulties arise where a name originally in a Western European language was transformed into Russian spelling, as for example César Cui, who was of partly French blood, and would seem very unfamiliar if transcribed back as "Tsezar Kiui" from the Cyrillic version. Some exceptions inevitably occur, therefore, but all text is given according to this book's transliteration system in reference to Russian publications in the footnotes (where Tchaikovsky appears as "Chaikovskii").

Dates are given throughout according to the Gregorian, or "New-Style" calendar (this has involved westernizing all dates for events occurring in Russia, which used the Julian, "Old-Style" calendar, running twelve days behind the Gregorian, in the nineteenth century).[3] Operas and other musical works throughout the book are given dates in parentheses, which relate, unless otherwise indicated, to the composition of the work concerned.

During the writing of this book, I have received assistance and encouragement from various people. I am grateful to Ann Lawrie and David Bubb for their personal support in the midst of difficult times, and to Mr. Bubb for providing considerable help with typing. The linguist, and author of studies on Tchaikovsky's operas, Philip Taylor, gave valuable advice on certain points. The Pushkin scholar Professor A.D.P. Briggs kindly checked the chapters on Tchaikovsky's Pushkin-based operas, *Eugene Onegin, Mazeppa* (which derives from the narrative poem *Poltava*), and *The Queen of Spades,* making some helpful suggestions. Nigel Gotteri and Professor Robert Russell of the Department of Russian and Slavonic Studies at Sheffield University helped resolve some difficult matters concerning translation from Russian. I am also grateful to Professors R.J. Wiley and Thomas Kohlhase; Mrs. Polina Vaidman, archivist at the State Tchaikovsky House-Museum at Klin (which kindly provided the photograph reproduced here from Tchaikovsky's musical sketches); Dr. Stuart Campbell; Mr. Vladimir Morosan; Tom McCanna, music librarian at Sheffield University; and staff at the Hammersmith Reference Library and Westminster Central Music Library, London. And, finally, I wish to thank William Morris for his help with proofreading.

Published editions of Tchaikovsky's operas form the basis of this text, and while every effort has been made to resolve discrepancies between these, no thorough overhaul has been attempted—an endeavor that would involve protracted research with primary source materials and that is beyond the scope of the present short study. There is, however, need for a fully revised edition of his operas, all the more as these works form a far more significant part of his achievement than is usually thought.

Tchaikovsky's great versatility as a composer, although apparent even from the fragment of his output that is established in regular performance, seems all the more remarkable when one looks into the spectrum of his neglected works. They show a restless creative spirit, and though, undeniably, there were phases of uncertainty, they seem merely to mark the transitions between the aftershocks of self-assurance that invigorated a compositional personality capable of mediating some seismically vital artistic process. The depth of what Tchaikovsky achieved as a composer has, I believe, only begun to be sensed. If I have managed to give some pointers to it here, I will not feel my efforts wasted.

Henry Zajaczkowski,
Mansfield, England

CHAPTER ONE

A SURVEY: TCHAIKOVSKY'S OPERAS AND THEIR HISTORICAL BACKGROUND

TCHAIKOVSKY ALWAYS CHERISHED an ambivalent hope to be successful as an opera composer. He sometimes seemed to look upon opera as a necessary evil, a genre whose popularity could gain a composer wide acclaim (as opposed to the more exclusive medium of, say, chamber music), and he considered his great German contemporary Johannes Brahms (1833–97), for whose work he felt deep antipathy, to be nevertheless a "hero" for attempting no operas. His own dramatic impulse was such a driving force in his symphonies, concertos, and single-movement orchestral works (indeed, even in his chamber music there is material, most notably in the Piano Trio, that could be described as "operatic") that his marrying of that impulse with the direct expression of words and an acted-out context on stage, in opera, formed a very natural outlet for his gifts. His range was broad. He completed ten operas, of which only one, his second, *Undine* (1869), was not actually produced on the stage. He eventually destroyed that work, reincorporating material from it into later compositions, a fate shared by his first opera, *The Voevoda* (1867–68), a tale of a lascivious provincial governor[1]—although Soviet scholars would eventually reconstruct the latter, with the result that, in total, nine performable operas by the composer exist. *Undine* was based on a fairytale, and fairytale aspects pertain also to his last opera, *Yolande* (1891), in which a blind princess regains her sight through the power of love. At the other extreme from those two works and Tchaikovsky's only comic opera, *Vakula the Smith* (which also has a fantastical theme, featuring the Devil besotted with a witch; 1874, revised 1885, and retitled *Cherevichki*), are the melodramas with a backdrop of Russian history: *The Oprichnik* (1870–72), concerning the reign of Ivan the Terrible, and *Mazeppa* (1881–83), which unfolds against the background of the clash between the rebel Ukrainian hetman of the work's title and Peter the Great. The plots of both these operas plumb a remarkable depth of tragic horror, almost unmitigated by any ray of hope, as too does the story of *The Enchantress* (1885–87), set in fifteenth-century Russia.

A number of revivals of Tchaikovsky's neglected operas in the final two decades of the twentieth century helped reveal their powerful qualities, perhaps the most remarkable revelation being the impact on stage of *The Maid of Orléans*[2] (a romanticized account of the events involving Joan of Arc), a work widely noted not only for an imperfect libretto, but also for an inflated, bombastic, and largely uninspired score. However, the determination Tchaikovsky showed in underlining the hysteria of a nation riven by internecine conflict as well as being under attack from another nation, through music that does not shun the openly hysterical as an artistic tool, but indeed fully explores it, is a mark of the strengths that he progressively acquired as a dramatist, of his recognition that purely musical dictates must sometimes be set aside in favor of the overall dramatic impact. *The Maid of Orléans* is one of his greatest works.[3] Anatoly Liadov once wrote, in admiration of Tchaikovsky's integrity as a creative artist and without any irony, of his "never fearing disapproval, never shunning commonplaces!"[4] (A similar lack of compositional doubts would perhaps have encouraged Liadov, whose output was comparatively small, to write more.) The greatest musical riches per se in Tchaikovsky's operas are in *Eugene Onegin,* which, unlike *The Maid of Orléans,* has a securely established place in the repertoire. Paradoxically, it was *The Maid* (1878–79, revised 1882), the immediate successor to *Onegin* (1877–78), that Tchaikovsky hoped would be the box-office hit, its grand-opera style being in marked distinction to the intimacies of *Onegin,* which had led him to designate that work merely "lyrical scenes" rather than a full-fledged opera.

The Queen of Spades (1890) embodies some of the deepest aspects of the composer's last period,[5] in which he gave eloquent voice to human suffering. It is an intricate psychological study of the descent of its hero, Hermann, into an apparently paranoid and delusional self-destruction. Although it is often criticized for failing to convey the ironical tone of the short story by Pushkin upon which it is based, the opera transmutes the original narrative into an artistic experience of equal dignity, and it so enables an audience to be moved by the human frailty of its hero as he passes into insanity that it corroborates Jung's bon mot "Show me a sane man and I will cure him for you." A distinguished conductor of one of the late twentieth-century revivals of Tchaikovsky's operas, Mark Elder, who conducted the English National Opera's production of *Mazeppa* at the Coliseum in London in December 1984 and January 1985, observed that he approached this extremely little-known work unable to believe that Tchaikovsky would "just happen to write two wonderful operas [i.e., *Eugene Onegin* and the other repertory mainstay, *The Queen of Spades*], but the rest you might as well forget."[6]

Tchaikovsky illumined more of the human condition in his operas than their prevailing neglect would seem to suggest.

The broad background to Tchaikovsky's, and other nineteenth-century Russian composers,' operatic achievement goes back to the preceding century. Russia's provincial status in relation to the more advanced European countries led to her being a late developer as concerns opera (and art-music in general). Italy cradled the very beginnings of opera as a genre, at the end of the sixteenth and the start of the seventeenth centuries, but it came to Russia only in the eighteenth century. It was, indeed, an Italian opera, a *commedia per musica* entitled *Calandro*, by Giovanni Ristori, that appears to be the first opera ever performed in Russia. Ristori's visiting opera company gave the work (which had already been premiered in Italy) in Moscow in 1731. Subsequently, a succession of Italian composers came to be employed at the imperial court in St. Petersburg, including Francesco Araja, whose *La forza dell'amore e dell'odio* was performed in 1736, and whose *Tsefal i Prokris* (*Cephalus and Procris*), with text by Alexander Sumarokov, premiered in 1755, claims title as the first opera to have been performed in Russian (and by Russian performers). The late eighteenth century saw a rapid and impressive development of true native opera (that is, by indigenous Russian composers), much of it incorporating the direct use of Russian folk music, as in *Pererozhdenie* (The Rebirth) by Dementy Zorin, first performed in 1777, the first entirely extant opera by a Russian composer.[7]

Not until the nineteenth century, however, did a composer of sufficient creative strength emerge to build the foundations for a distinct and idiosyncratic tradition of national Russian opera to develop. Mikhail Glinka (1804–57) was the first composer of world stature to be produced by Russia. His most important works were his two operas, *A Life for the Tsar* (1834–36) and *Ruslan and Liudmila* (1837–42), and, profoundly dichotomous although they were—the former a forceful and effective drama, the latter weak and disorganized as drama, but rich in the most fertile musical invention[8]—they molded, to varying degrees, the operatic output of composers as diverse as Alexander Dargomyzhsky (1813–69), Tchaikovsky himself, and his contemporaries, the members of the so-called "Mighty Handful." The Mighty Handful was an informal affiliation of composers comprising Nikolai Rimsky-Korsakov (1844–1908), César Cui (1835–1918), Modest Musorgsky (1839–81), Alexander Borodin (1833–87), and their autocratic leader (the only member of the group, however, who wrote no operas) Mily Balakirev (1837–1910). Although there has been much critical focus on the differences between the conservatoire-trained (and therefore strongly Western-influenced) Tchaikovsky, and the largely self-taught and avowedly nationalist Mighty Handful, the stylistic demarcation between them is much more blurred than is usually supposed. Tchaikovsky's full formal training did not induce in him any tentativeness whatsoever as to assimilating the adventurous, indeed, avant-garde aspects of Glinka's work, which the Balakirev group also eagerly absorbed. Nor did Tchaikovsky show any unwillingness to enrich his works with Russian folk-influence, whose widespread presence in his music up to the mid-1870s is one of its most conspicuous characteristics. Even after that time, as we shall see, it was an important (although less frequent) factor. Indeed, all in all, Tchaikovsky learned no less from Glinka than did any of his compatriots. In *A Life for the Tsar,* Glinka employed substantial Russian folk-influence as a vehicle for setting the story of Ivan Susanin, the peasant who in 1612 or 1613 gave his life to save the first Romanov tsar, by guiding a group of Polish soldiers, on a mission to capture him, away from their quarry. Just as significant as the overall absorption of folk-based style is the innovation of the opera having a tragic ending, enhanced by that stylistic context. Previous Russian operas had avoided tragic denouements by means of sudden rescues, or the device of the "deus ex machina," the appearance of a benign deity who prevents the impending calamity. Here the hero actually dies, and the nobility of his self-sacrifice for his country's sake is conveyed with cathartic strength by the use of Russian folk style for his aria "They guess the truth"[9] in Act 4, when he knows the Poles will shortly kill him for deceiving them. A contemporary commentator, Prince Vladimir Odoevsky, observed that this opera constituted a historic turning point, as it proved that "Russian melody . . . may be elevated to the level of tragedy."[10] To have secured this achievement at this point in his nation's artistic development was particularly significant, for Glinka finished composing *A Life for the Tsar* in the same year that Italian opera, which had suddenly fallen into decline in Russia at the start of the nineteenth century, dramatically regained ascendancy, starting with the production of Rossini's *Semiramide* in St. Petersburg in 1836. Glinka revealed the noble spirit of peasant music at the same time that the suave sophistication of Italian opera returned to the fore.

In an entirely different way, *Ruslan and Liudmila* was also an antidote to Italian opera (despite the presence in it, as in *A Life for the Tsar*, of various aspects of Italian operatic style). Its technical innovations were astonishing; for instance, Glinka devised as one of the opera's dances a barbaric *Lezginka* that, as David Brown suggests, displays such "elemental rhythms, brilliant colours, harsh counterpoints, and [such a] daemonic end, [that it] must surely have been the most advanced piece of European music of its time."[11] Glinka also invented an artificial musical scale for use at specific points in the opera, the whole-tone scale,[12] which is highly disruptive of the sense of key and which predates its more famous use by the French composer Claude Debussy (1862–1918) by half a century. This was a means of depicting the opera's villain, the evil dwarf Chernomor, and his magical powers. The plot, adapted from Pushkin's fairytale poem, concerns Chernomor's abduction of the heroine just as she is about to be wed and the hero's adventures in rescuing her. Russian folk style is less prominent here than in *A Life for the Tsar* (where it had alternated with Polish dance music to represent the rival national factions), for it now appears as part of a whole series of ethnic musical evocations, alongside Tatar, Caucasian, Persian, Arab, Turkish, and Finnish.

Tchaikovsky was spiritually more drawn to *A Life for the Tsar* than to *Ruslan and Liudmila*, although he was indebted to the latter whenever he had to evoke a magical or supernatural idiom or to depict evil (whether supernatural or otherwise). Indeed, references to that work abound not only in his operas but occur elsewhere too—for example the use of the whole-tone scale in *Swan Lake* and the *Manfred* Symphony.[13] Even so, he never embraced *Ruslan and Liudmila*'s influence to the extent displayed in Borodin's opera *Prince Igor* (begun 1869, still unfinished at the composer's death in 1887, completed by Rimsky-Korsakov and Glazunov), in which a Polovtsian (i.e., Tatar) khan takes captive the Russian prince of the work's title. The oriental musical idiom developed by Glinka in the *Persian Chorus* (sung by seductive maidens at the palace of the sorceress Naina), the *Lezginka*, and the songs of the oriental Prince Ratmir in *Ruslan and Liudmila,* are the progenitors of the *Polovtsian Dances* and the music sung by Khan Konchak's daughter in Borodin's work, and also, for example, Cleopatra's seductive dance and the *Indian Dance* in Rimsky-Korsakov's opera-ballet *Mlada* (1889–90). These are colorful blossoms on the oriental tree that Glinka planted, but in which Tchaikovsky showed only slight interest.

Tchaikovsky wrote some superbly evocative ballet-music entertainments in the course of his operas, but he never used the oriental idiom in that context, and was in general less drawn to it than were Borodin and Rimsky-Korsakov. However, in the field of ballet proper he did employ orientalism briefly: in the celebrated *Arabian Dance*, based on a Georgian lullaby, and the fleeting *Chinese Dance*, in Act 2 of *The Nutcracker* (1891–92). That ballet was written to appear as a double bill with *Yolande* in which, for the first time in any of his operas, Tchaikovsky made use of the oriental manner. As he was to compose no further operas, the music sung by the minor character, the Moorish physician Ibn Yahya, was also his last operatic foray into orientalism. Here it is the wisdom of the physician, who is entrusted with curing Yolande's blindness, that is emphasized by the use of that musical idiom, rather than any notably colorful effect. Perhaps Tchaikovsky felt the utilization of Glinka's oriental gestures à la *Ruslan* brought with it an inevitable baggage of associations with that work, something that might detract from the seriousness of the kind of opera that he preferred to write (and which indeed typifies *A Life for the Tsar*), in which people's feelings, rather than the colorfulness of the story's location and character types, are emphasized. Although he was prepared to compose an opera and a ballet to be performed in the same evening as separate, but mutually complementary, entities, Tchaikovsky never tried to combine the two types of drama organically, for, unlike Rimsky-Korsakov, he had no sympathy with "opera-ballet" as a genre, viewing it as a rather vague hybrid.

CHAPTER TWO

UNCERTAIN BEGINNINGS: THE VOEVODA *AND* UNDINE

TCHAIKOVSKY'S FIRST OPERA had an inauspicious start, for although the writing of the libretto, based on the play *The Voevoda*, was initially undertaken by none other than its author, Ostrovsky, Tchaikovsky was unfortunate enough to lose the first installment, Act 1. The playwright graciously wrote it out again for the young composer from memory, but, understandably cooling toward the project, wrote little more, adding only the text of Act 2 scene 1 and the words for Maria's song about the nightingale in the following scene. Tchaikovsky had to write the rest of the libretto himself. The original plan, as agreed with Ostrovsky, had been to condense the play (subtitled *a Dream on The Volga*), which had five Acts and a prologue, into four Acts, but when the playwright retreated from the project, Tchaikovsky completed the libretto in a format of three Acts in total. The plot, set in the mid-seventeenth century, runs as follows:

Act 1:   A large town by the Volga; the garden at the home of the wealthy merchant Diuzhoi. Shalygin, the Voevoda (provincial governor of military rank), who is betrothed to Diuzhoi's elder daughter Praskovia, visits Diuzhoi, and noticing her younger sister Maria, takes a sudden preference to her. Maria's beloved is a young nobleman, Bastriukov. Ironically, just prior to Shalygin's arrival, Bastriukov with a group of servants had broken through the fence into Diuzhoi's garden to see Maria; he had tried to persuade her to come away with him for fear that Shalygin, his enemy, would use his influence, through marriage to Praskovia, to prevent his own intended marriage to Maria. After presently confronting Bastriukov, the Voevoda takes Maria with him against her will.

Act 2 scene 1:   The entrance hall at Bastriukov's house. A visitor, Dubrovin, comes and relates how he too had been tyrannized by Shalygin who, two years previously, had abducted his wife Olëna, caused his ruin, and outlawed him. Dubrovin discloses that the Voevoda is due to set off on a pilgrimage the next day, which provides a chance to rescue their two loved ones.

Act 2 scene 2: [The Voevoda's home.] Maria sings of a nightingale that holds to its freedom rather than accept the offer of life in a golden cage. The plans for the escape are conveyed to Maria by Olëna.

Act 3: A courtyard with at one side a tower and staircase. All goes well with the rescue at first, but the lovers celebrate their immediate reunion too long, lingering within the bounds of the Voevoda's residence; he now returns and recaptures them. He says he will kill Maria, forces her offstage, and just when the situation is at its gravest, a new Voevoda providentially arrives to replace the old one.

The Voevoda,[1] composed from 1867 to 1868, was first performed at the Bolshoi Theater in Moscow on 11 February 1869, conducted by Eduard Merten. Despite its dramatic weaknesses, it contains a wealth of lyrical beauty that is only surpassed by that of *Eugene Onegin*. The composition of the first work of a particular genre typically roused Tchaikovsky to an acute warmth of lyrical feeling, as evinced also in the First Symphony (whose slow movement's sense of a heart worn on the sleeve is only matched by the Fifth Symphony's second movement), the B flat minor Piano Concerto's soaring melodic qualities (which are quite unparalleled by its two successors), and *Swan Lake,* which, though less great than *The Sleeping Beauty* and, even more notably, *The Nutcracker*, nevertheless exceeds both in terms of its capacity to move the listener by melody alone. The music in E major marking the point at which Bastriukov is reunited with Maria, and Dubrovin with Olëna, during the rescue (and before Shalygin's return) in Act 3 of *The Voevoda*, was reused in *Swan Lake* for Prince Siegfried's stressful reunion with Odette, when he comes rushing onstage at the start of the final scene. It exemplifies Tchaikovsky's melodic gift at its greatest.

Although it is influenced by both of Glinka's operas, *The Voevoda* is mainly under the aegis of *A Life for the Tsar*. This is shown preeminently in the extensive use of Russian folk style. Although only three actual folk songs have been identified in *The Voevoda* (the tally being similar, interestingly enough, to that in *A Life for the Tsar*, where it appears that either two or three authentic folk melodies were used),[2] it seems Tchaikovsky had an ability that was closely comparable to Glinka's to compose new melodies in the folk idiom, and in these *The Voevoda* abounds. In this respect Tchaikovsky can be deemed to have been truly a Russian nationalist, for while the folkloristic influence upon his music greatly diminishes after its climax in *Vakula the Smith*—being incorporated thereafter, through a particularly expressive kind of juxtaposition, into his broader, cosmopolitan style—he proved himself in his early works to be a fully worthy successor to Glinka in terms of emulating folk music.

Moreover, for any composer working within the genres and style of Western art-music—as both Tchaikovsky and the Mighty Handful did—the use of a Russian folk song raises some challenging difficulties. These had already been addressed by Glinka, whose methods for dealing with them were keenly adopted by his aforementioned successors, who seemed, in so aligning themselves with the "father of Russian music" (who is worthy of the title, as he found effective creative routes through which native music could be introduced into the art-music field) to be emphasizing their Russian credentials. That appears as important a factor in determining what Russian nationalism is as the use of actual indigenous folk songs, or the ability to compose a folk-like melody. The main compositional problem was that a folk theme is a fully worked and self-contained organism in its own right and does not readily lend itself to development in the Western sense. To obviate this, Glinka formulated a technique of changing-background variations (with roots in folk practice, but developed to a high degree of Western-style sophistication) in which the folk melody (or one written by the composer in the folk mold) is brilliantly paraded by being constantly repeated, each time with a different accompaniment, thereby passing through a shifting panorama of textures and coloration. He employed the method to its fullest effect in his orchestral piece *Kamarinskaia*, with notable antecedents in the *Persian Chorus*[3] from *Ruslan* and the *Slavsia* chorus (which, like *Kamarinskaia*, Tchaikovsky revered) which welcomes the new Tsar to Moscow at the end of *A Life for the Tsar*. The folk songs used in *The Voevoda* are "On the sea a duckling was bathing" (which appears as the girls' chorus at the start of Act 1), "My plait, my little plait" (Maria's song in Act 2 scene 2, which Tchaikovsky set to Ostrovsky's metaphorically apt text about a nightingale preferring its freedom to the offer of life in a golden cage), and "Beyond the courtyard is a little meadow, a little green meadow" (girls' *Khorovod*—a round-dance with choral singing—at the end of Act 2 scene 2).[4] Tchaikovsky treats all three to changing-background variations, following Glinka's precedent.

Furthermore, the opening theme of the Overture, and much melodic material in the *Entr'acte and Dance of the Serving-Maids* at the start of Act 2 scene 2,[5] these being melodies composed in folk style by Tchaikovsky, are also presented in changing-background variation form. The technique was used by Tchaikovsky with no less sensitivity to nuance than that shown by his avowedly nationalist rivals—as, for example, in the *Khorovod of the Rusalki* (mermaids) in Act 3 of *May Night* (1878–79) by Rimsky-Korsakov.

The coda to *The Voevoda*'s Overture, which reappears in the opera itself as the jubilant final chorus, is reminiscent of the chorus in honor of the Love-God, Lel, in Act 1 of *Ruslan and Liudmila*, both in terms of the contours of the melody and the use of unorthodox meter. Tchaikovsky here writes in an alternation of three-beat and five-beat measures, echoing the setting of Glinka's chorus in quintuple time. Western art-music was conventionally cast in constant quadruple, triple, duple, or (less commonly) sextuple meter, and the metrical structures he and Glinka used in these instances are very alien to it. Glinka broadened the art-music framework with a bold ethnic influence, for quintuple time is a characteristic of Russian wedding folk songs (the chorus from *Ruslan* occurs as part of the nuptial festivities, just prior to the abduction of Liudmila; Glinka had already written a bridal chorus in five-time in Act 3 of *A Life for the Tsar*). Although Tchaikovsky never explored the unconventional use of meter as deeply as Borodin did in *Song of the Dark Forest* (1868), with its extraordinarily restless shifts between a range of meters,[6] nevertheless he was, on various further occasions, fully willing to break Western convention to felicitous effect—as in the beautiful quintuple-meter girls' chorus at the start of *Mazeppa*.

Ruslan's influence appears also, for example, in a brief passage based on the whole-tone scale, here depicting human, rather than supernatural, evil. The D major fanfare that heralds the appearance of the new Voevoda at the end of the opera, and deliverance, marks a reassertion of the orthodox use of keys after the subversiveness of the four measures of (Chernomor-inspired) whole-tone-system music that immediately precede it and that mark the work's darkest moment, when Maria has been forced offstage by the old Voevoda, who has threatened to kill her. Musically, therefore, the arrival of Shalygin's successor is handled effectively, however disappointingly facile this symbolic deus ex machina is as a resolver of the action of an opera that contains such little dramatic incident. Perhaps Glinka's second opera also had an effect on *The Voevoda's* orchestration, which is highly colorful and variegated, although this may have been one of the features Tchaikovsky had in mind when, a decade after the premiere, he observed to his patroness Mrs. von Meck that in *The Voevoda* he had been "mainly concerned with filigree-work and quite forgot the stage and all its conditions."[7] Such scoring may, at times, detract from what is happening on stage, although it would certainly be among this work's distinguishing qualities if it were given in concert performance.

Whereas condensation of a play is almost always vital if it is to form a good libretto (as the sung word lasts longer than the spoken one), that to which Ostrovsky's original text was submitted was injudiciously done in circumstances that, as we saw, were regrettable. It produced the bare bones of a drama, rather than a fully viable one, and it is perhaps not surprising that Tchaikovsky produced very little characterization in the opera (i.e., music designed to distinguish the various characters from each other by means of some musical features peculiarly suited to each). The only real exception to this is the music Tchaikovsky allotted to Dubrovin, the figure whose plight is all the more moving through his shouldering the injustices placed upon him by the Voevoda without the privileges of social rank enjoyed by the aristocrat Bastriukov. Dubrovin can therefore stand more easily as a symbol of humanity's suffering. Brown mentions the parallels between the "capacity which Dubrovin shares with both of Glinka's heroes (and, it seems, with the Russian people in general) for quiet, heroic endurance,"[8] and he identifies a short, strongly folk-like melody associated with Dubrovin as the sole example of "anything which might be termed a leitmotif in the whole opera."[9] That particular melody recurs repeatedly in the opera, in other words, as a kind of musical tag characterizing Dubrovin. The use of leitmotifs (the term itself was initially employed regarding the operas of the German composer Carl Maria von Weber [1786–1826]) was commonplace in opera composition by the time of the writing of Tchaikovsky's first opera, but Tchaikovsky was surely, in this instance, harking back to Susanin's great aria in Act 4 of *A Life for the Tsar* ("They guess the truth") where, as he anticipates his impending death, he recalls a series of themes associated with members of his family. Tchaikovsky would explore leitmotifs further in later operas, along with the general reuse of musical material among the scenes. His specific use of leitmotif here recaptures a little of the emotional power connected with Glinka's peasant hero.

Tchaikovsky's later probing into the expressive and dramatic potential of leitmotifs did not, however, lead him to adopt them, as certain of his contemporaries did, as a fully systemized method for establishing characterization and the interaction between characters in an opera. For example, although he would make effective use of a number of leitmotifs in *The Oprichnik*, he would never use them as the main means of articulating the overall dramatic structure of an opera, unlike Musorgsky in *Boris Godunov* (whose revised version, of 1871–72, while less saturated with leitmotifs than the original, of 1868–69, nevertheless makes bold use of the leitmotif ethic). Tchaikovsky had, moreover, no sympathy whatsoever with the revolution in operatic structure that was brought about by the German composer Richard Wagner (1813–83), in which the absolutely rigorous application of leitmotifs led to a continuous texture of symphonic interaction in an opera, even sweeping aside the standard division of the work into choruses, arias, duets, trios, and so on. The Acts of a mature Wagner opera each unfold like a single tapestry, rather than being, in the format that he rejected, a series of paintings in a gallery. But Tchaikovsky's compositional style always tended more to the juxtapositional than the integrative,[10] and, although Gerald Abraham was certainly right to state that Tchaikovsky was "content to take, and leave, the conventions of Victorian opera as he found them,"[11] it should be emphasized that in doing so he enriched the old format with music that transcended its banality.

One of the most well-known remarks about Tchaikovsky's operas is Abraham's comment, concerning *The Oprichnik*, that it is "Meyerbeer translated into Russian."[12] He added that it is "very thoroughly translated."[13] But the French grand-opera tradition, most famously displayed in the operas of the German-Jewish composer Giacomo Meyerbeer (1791–1864) (who wrote operas in French, for production in Paris) was translated by Tchaikovsky not just very thoroughly into Russian, but into the expressive framework of his own unique style, as we shall presently see. *The Oprichnik* was Tchaikovsky's third opera, but it was the first to reach us fully intact.

Several fragments only have survived from Tchaikovsky's second opera. *Undine* was even less fortunate than *The Voevoda*, which, because it had at least been given a stage production, bequeathed an archival set of performing parts which aided the scholars who reconstructed the score, largely bypassing the composer's action in destroying it. His destruction of *Undine*, however, was preceded by its failure to be granted performance by the directorate of the Imperial Theaters in St. Petersburg, to whom it was submitted in its year of composition, 1869 (a corresponding set of parts was therefore not even prepared). The libretto, after Friedrich de la Motte Fouqué, is about the jealous love of the eponymous heroine, a water sprite, for a mortal, the knight Huldbrand, and her foiling of his marriage to Berthalda. The wedding march became the Second Symphony's second movement. A love duet for Undine and Huldbrand was adapted for reuse in what would be one of *Swan Lake*'s most famous numbers, the great G flat major dance for the Prince and Odette in Act 2.

After *Undine* Tchaikovsky was briefly attracted to *Mandragora*, a tale by a professor of botany, Sergei Rachinsky, about a magical plant transformed into a beautiful maiden, but composed only a *Chorus of Flowers and Insects* (1870) for this abortive opera. He was dissuaded from further work on it by his friend and Moscow Conservatoire colleague Nikolai Kashkin, who felt the story more appropriate for a ballet.

CHAPTER THREE

FRESH IMPETUS:
THE OPRICHNIK

WITH *THE OPRICHNIK,* Tchaikovsky stands revealed as a highly potent and insightful musical dramatist. Whereas *The Voevoda*'s libretto had provided little framework for such skills to be seen, that of *The Oprichnik,* adapted by the composer himself from Ivan Lazhechnikov's tragedy (which was entitled *The Oprichniks*), provided much. The strong situations and the composer's willingness to emphasize their climaxes with uncompromisingly dynamic music were the legacy not only of Meyerbeer's operas but also those of the influential, though now almost forgotten, Russian composer Alexander Serov (1820–71), whose *Judith*, premiered in 1863, Tchaikovsky deeply esteemed. Andrei Morozov, the hero of Tchaikovsky's opera, through force of circumstance joins the *oprichniks*, the vicious, special cohorts of Ivan the Terrible. They were established in 1565 (remaining in operation for some seven years), policing the Tsar's bizarre, artificial division of the nation into two realms: his own territory, appropriated, with some bloodshed, from the *boiars* (or nobility), who were reallocated land for their own governance. Andrei is, however, himself a member of the boiar class. The action unfolds as follows:

Act 1: Moscow; Prince Zhemchuzhny's garden. Zhemchuzhny allocates his daughter Natalia's hand in marriage, without dowry, to Mitkov, a delighted elderly suitor. Both exit.

Natalia, her nurse Zakharevna, and a group of girls singing a folk chorus enter. Forlorn, Natalia sings about a nightingale that holds freedom dearer than an offer to live in a golden cage. They exit.

Natalia's beloved, Andrei Morozov, and some oprichniks led by Basmanov, a favorite of the Tsar, break through the fence into Zhemchuzhny's garden. Andrei tells Basmanov he will become an oprichnik, to be avenged on

Zhemchuzhny for robbing and driving his family from their home. More-over, he will not give up his betrothed. Basmanov lends him money and advises him not to see Natalia yet, but instead hurry to his mother for her blessing, then to the Tsar's domain (to take the oprichnik's oath). They exit.

Natalia, thinking she heard Andrei, rushes in, but too late to see him. She displays her longing for him in an arioso. Zakharevna and the girls return and, to raise Natalia's spirits, perform a khorovod.

Act 2 scene 1: A peasant's hut. The old noblewoman Morozova, Andrei's mother, feels her degradation by Zhemchuzhny was God's will, and she prays that the Almighty protect her son. Enter Andrei, who hands her the oprichnik Basmanov's money. Horrified, she demands he return it, but accepts it when he commends a sworn assurance that Basmanov gave, that he received it from Andrei's father as a comrade-in-arms. She begs Andrei to return peace to his dead father, and he vows, "I shall wash away the bloody insult."

Anxious that Andrei might be drawn into following Basmanov into the oprichniks, Morozova tells him not to fraternize with him. She weeps. Andrei tells her he will not trespass against her wishes—but adds, in an aside, that so as to eradicate the insult, he must deceive her. She asks him not to leave her lonely with her bitter fate—to live without him would be hard. Andrei says a voice like his father's calls for vengeance from the grave. She gives him her blessing before he departs.

Act 2 scene 2: The Tsar's settlement [to the northeast of Moscow]. Two choruses sung by oprichniks frame the scene: the opening one (offstage) in Russian liturgical style, the closing one a triumphal rendering of the oprichniks' leitmotif. Between them, Andrei is sworn in as an oprichnik by Prince Viazminsky, an enemy of his late father. Basmanov attempts to per-suade Viazminsky to forget his enmity for the Morozovs. Andrei confesses that he joins the oprichniks through sheer necessity. During the oath he stands with the oprichniks' blades at his head. He must forgo all ties with the landowning class—which places him in an impossible position because he must disown his mother, and also, in effect, himself. Viazminsky insists that he actually renounce his mother. Basmanov shouts acceptance over Andrei's shoulder, but Andrei refutes this as Satan's voice. "Swear, or death awaits you!" exclaim Viazminsky and the chorus of oprichniks. Andrei agonizes, then cries, "To hell with everything! I swear!"

Act 3: A square in Moscow. The townsfolk feel deserted by the Tsar (who has withdrawn to the seclusion of his settlement outside the city) in the midst of evil times. Morozova, with a sense of foreboding, goes toward the church to pray, but a gang of boys taunts her, to her astonishment, as a "filthy oprichnik" (she is not yet aware of Andrei's actions). Natalia appears and runs to Morozova begging for her protection; she has run away from her father, unable to bear him or the man to whom he has granted permission to wed her. They now both approach the church, afraid that Zhemchuzhny may apprehend them. He indeed arrives with his servants, scorns Morozova's attempt to intercede on Natalia's behalf, and is about to have his defiant daughter tied up when Andrei, Basmanov, and a group of fellow oprichniks arrive. Appalled that her son is among oprichniks, Morozova asks him to explain. He avows that he joined them to answer his father's plea from the grave for revenge, and that he remains true to her. He is ominously warned by the oprichniks to observe his oath. His mother replies that it was Satan's voice, not her husband's, that Andrei heard, and she lays her curse on him, thereby disowning the son she loves. Amid general shock, Basmanov proposes that they return, with Natalia and Morozova, to see the Tsar, in the hope that he may release Andrei from his oath. Then, all will be as in a dream.

Act 4: The Tsar's settlement. At the start of the Act, which opens with a wedding chorus in honor of Andrei and Natalia, all their troubles seem to be over. The Tsar has released Andrei from his oath, returned Natalia to him, and confounded Zhemchuzhny. However, there is a caveat: Andrei is to remain an oprichnik until midnight. Basmanov cautions his friend to remember that. Natalia feels increasing dread at the continued feasting. After the third time that the wedding chorus is heard, Basmanov brings grave news. A storm is breaking, with Andrei at the center. There has been plotting against him, compounded by his own madness in using the oprichniks to regain his status, then forgetting all about that. Basmanov solemnly advises loyalty to the oprichniks' oath, but Andrei does not understand him. Viazminsky enters. He tells Andrei the Tsar wishes to see his bride—of whose beauty he has heard—in private. Andrei cannot hide his outrage. Natalia faints. Andrei curses the Tsar. Viazminsky orders Natalia to be taken to the Tsar, with whom Basmanov unsuccessfully pleads on his friend's behalf. Viazminsky commands that Andrei be led to execution, then brings in Morozova. She sees the evil gleam in his eye and demands to know where Andrei is. She screams and drops down dead as she sees her son being put to death. An offstage chorus of oprichniks praises the Tsar.

The Oprichnik, composed from 1870 to 1872, was premiered at the Mariinsky Theater in St. Petersburg on 24 April 1874, conducted by Eduard Nápravník. The combination of the macrocosm of turbulent times in history and the microcosm of personal tragedies played out against it was a winning formula in French grand opera. Meyerbeer's *Les Huguenots*, premiered in 1836, to a libretto by Eugène Scribe and Emile Deschamps, with which *The Oprichnik* has often been compared, was the first opera to be given over one thousand performances at the Paris Opéra. But despite initial success, *The Oprichnik* gradually fell into obscurity during the composer's lifetime and has not recovered since.[1] Its long-term chances of success were damaged by Tchaikovsky himself: during the rehearsals for the premiere, he developed a profound antipathy toward this opera. His aversion was fueled (in addition to purely musical or dramaturgical concerns) by his detestation of V. V. Bessel, who published *The Oprichnik* and to whom he ceded the rights to the opera. He felt Bessel had taken advantage of him financially, and he wished to deny the publisher any future income from performance royalties. Tchaikovsky eventually declared an intention to revise the opera (but never did so) and was outraged when *The Oprichnik* was revived in the Panaev Theater in St. Petersburg in 1890, even recommending his main publisher, Jürgenson (a powerful rival of Bessel's), to commence legal action against the theater to safeguard his wishes as composer. The performances ceased.[2]

There are a number of correlations between *Les Huguenots* and *The Oprichnik*, including the remoteness of historical setting. The story of Meyerbeer's opera unfolds at much the same period as Tchaikovsky's, but against the background of an actual historical event, the massacre in Paris on St Bartholomew's Day in 1572 of over 3,000 Huguenots (French Protestants). In Tchaikovsky's work, Andrei Morozov takes an oath (in Act 2 scene 2) to join Ivan the Terrible's oprichniks, persecutors of the nobility, to gain vengeance on Prince Zhemchuzhny; in Meyerbeer's opera, a Catholic nobleman, the Comte de Nevers, refuses to join a Catholic conspiracy in the scene of the blessing of the daggers (in Act 4) to carry out the killing of the Protestants. Both scenes use religious mystique for stage effect: the chorus of oprichniks, who wear monk-like apparel (as part of the Tsar's strange regimen), at the start of the scene intone an offstage chant in ecclesiastical style, which switches repeatedly between a pair of chords to somewhat hypnotic effect; in Meyerbeer's work, the Comte de Saint-Bris and three monks administer the oath, to the Catholics who will perform the massacre, accompanied by a mystically alternating pair of harmonies. Although Meyerbeer's pair of chords exude a Western feel (one of them is chromatic, i.e., it does not belong to the prevailing key, A flat major) and Tchaikovsky's belong to one of the scale systems of Russian liturgical music (the aeolian mode), the expressive aims are similar and there is a notable technical resemblance (in both cases the alternation is between harmonies whose roots are a third apart), which points to an influence of Meyerbeer's upon his successor.

Act 4 of Meyerbeer's opera also includes the great love-duet, whose slow section, in G flat major, in which the Protestant hero, Raoul, sings "Tu l'as dit: oui, tu m'aimes!" is often noted as having had a shaping effect on Natalia's similarly impassioned and finely melodically molded arioso, in the same key, in Act 1 of *The Oprichnik*. Natalia's arioso is part of the very small quantity of music in Act 1 that is newly composed, as the bulk of that Act consists of material transferred from *The Voevoda*. Much of the criticism of *The Oprichnik* has concerned the reuse in it of music and verbal text from *The Voevoda*, and seminal to that criticism have been Modest Tchaikovsky's observations in his biography of his brother. Modest condemned the "violent intrusion of

Ostrovsky's text into [the composer's adaptation of] Lazhechnikov's tragedy [which] produced a distortion of the scenario and had a damaging effect on the entire libretto. The exposition became unclear, the characterization was utterly destroyed, beginning with the sly and avaricious Zhemchuzhny. At the rise of the curtain [the composer-librettist] has him chatting congenially with Mitkov and there is little trace of that maliciousness and cruelty which justifies Morozov's entrance into the *oprichnina* [the Tsar's domain]."[3] The scene between Zhemchuzhny and Mitkov was transferred from Act 1 of *The Voevoda*, where Diuzhoi convivially welcomes his future son-in-law, Shalygin, to his home (i.e., before the situation turns sour). Although Tchaikovsky did indeed severely weaken Zhemchuzhny's role as villain here, as also in his too-brief appearance in the rest of the opera (the remainder of his part being entirely confined to his small number of lines in Act 3), and partly filled that vacuum with the grossly evil Viazminsky (whose one-sidedness comes across almost as caricature),[4] Tchaikovsky showed a much firmer dramatic sense than Modest acknowledged. The first Act, whereas it displays little dramatic exposition of the plot per se and is largely decorative and lyrical in its music, works as a foil, and perhaps also a necessary counterbalance, to the unleashing of dramatic power in the rest of the opera. (That lyricism is, however, matched with an apt reuse of Ostrovsky's words in Natalia's song of the nightingale that prefers to be free rather than live in a golden cage, for here Tchaikovsky transferred Maria's song from Act 2 scene 2 of *The Voevoda*, reflecting the general dramatic context of a young woman denied her true love by the intercession of an older man—the malign Shalygin in Maria's case, the innocuous Mitkov in Natalia's.) The often raw dramatic force in Act 2 scene 2 when Andrei, seemingly entrapped by his own need for revenge, commits himself to the oprichniks' oath, and is also coerced by them into accepting it, the terrible strength of his mother's cursing and disowning of him in Act 3, and the cold and devastating power of Act 4, where Andrei and his mother lose their lives and his beloved Natalia is left to some unspecified fate at the Tsar's hands, gain all the more effect from the largely dissociated beauties of Act 1.

Echoing a critique advocated by Modest, Abraham noted that because Tchaikovsky wished to reemploy the music of Bastriukov's Act 1 entrance in *The Voevoda* as that of Andrei in Act 1 here—"the parallel being that each is a young lover breaking into a garden to see his sweetheart"—*The Oprichnik*'s hero is "made to break in violently [into Zhemchuzhny's garden] with his violent friends instead of creeping in alone and unobtrusively as in Lazhechnikov's play."[5] Modest felt that that is "against the very idea of the tragedy"[6] because we do not gain a due sense of Andrei's reluctance in joining the oprichniks but have our first impression of the hero as being hand-in-glove with them. Hermann Laroche criticized the music accompanying Andrei and his cohorts in this scene (which originally accompanied Bastriukov and his

servants in Act 1 of *The Voevoda*) as being like "overtures or finales sometimes written for comic operas."[7] Indeed, there is a somewhat Rossinian
quality to the hectic patter of the rhythmic figuration in the orchestra here.
The comical atmosphere was considered inappropriate by Laroche, as he
believed that what the composer had wished to convey was a sense of the
danger of the lovers being discovered in an impending encounter. The
incongruity of the music, however, clashing (as it also did in *The Voevoda*)
with the prevailing Russian folk-based idiom of the score, is much more
effective as a dramatic stratagem here than it had been in the earlier work.
Here it portrays a manic, mentally dissociated state experienced by Andrei as
he engages in the tragic hero's act of overreaching, an action that portends
his downfall (rather than Bastriukov's deed, which merely engages him as
part of a rather uneventful drama).

Taruskin has shown how strongly influenced Tchaikovsky was in con-
structing the libretto of *The Oprichnik* by the structural methods of Scribe
(French grand opera's foremost librettist, who wrote the libretti of several of
Meyerbeer's operas and also of those of a range of other composers). Focus-
ing on the climactic design of Act 3, he reveals it as a "classic Scribian act"[8]
formed to build up in atmosphere from a rather static opening chorus (here
the chorus of townsfolk bemoan their sense of desertion by the Tsar) and a
static solo arioso (here Morozova bemoans her own lonely fate and a sense
of impending doom) to a series of entrances of other characters,[9] each bringing a new and irreversible plot development. The whole leads to a confrontation and finale in which the resulting mood—both powerful yet strangely
static, there being no dramatic development while it is asserted—is "fixed
and monumentalized at length by the impressive music"[10] performed by
massed forces. Here comes the great quartet and chorus of pained astonishment sung in response to Morozova's renunciation of her own son.

This is modeled at the start, as Taruskin observes, on the quartet that follows Liudmila's abduction in Act 1 of *Ruslan and Liudmila*. The characters are
bound together in a loosely canonic treatment, the melody passing rather
mechanically between them, starting with Andrei (singing "I cannot yet
understand the meaning of her terrible words"), followed by Natalia and
Basmanov singing together, then Zhemchuzhny (whose words, however, are
different; he is preoccupied with his own predicament in the oprichniks'
presence), the overall atmosphere being of something trapped within itself.
The music, in D minor and in triple time, is underpinned by a tonic pedal,
which has the obsessive feature of the D sounding on the same weak pulse
(the second beat) from measure to measure. Again the derivation is from
Glinka's original (where an E flat had appeared in each measure's second
beat) and, also as in the original, the suppressive feel intensifies as the music
progresses. But here Tchaikovsky releases the accumulated tension into
something subtly propulsive, in other words, with an element of suppression

still present despite the sense of release.[11] The lengthy tonic pedal is suddenly transformed into a dominant preparation for the emergence of the new key, G minor, and a new melody in which, however, the tone D has a vital role. Its repetitions are not now so obsessive: It no longer sounds like a funereal knell in measure after measure on the second beat, but moves freely into different locations within each measure. Also, this new melody is not presented in canonic form: It is unfettered in that respect. Furthermore, the former pedal tone has emerged from the depths to float on the surface in the new melody, free of its former pedal function. The D nevertheless is stated repeatedly, insistently enough to signify that matters remain unresolved. To this melody Natalia sings, "No! No, it is no dream, a mother curses her own son!" Her words are taken up by the other soloists and the choral forces.

In music such as this, Tchaikovsky achieves an elevation of opera itself to a kind of metaphor of mankind's anguish and helplessness in the face of *force majeure,* and at the same time, through the intensity of his gift as a melodist, he expounds hope. He was thus able to embody in artistic terms Spinoza's dictum that there is no fear without hope and no hope without fear. Tchaikovsky's use of a lyrical ensemble-chorus simultaneously to fix a mood and provide some sense that that mood might be healed follows the definitive assertion of matters of principle by the opera's characters. Morozova here asserts family and personal pride above all else by disowning her son (whom she feels has betrayed the family honor and herself by joining the Tsar's bloodthirsty henchmen). Similarly, in *Eugene Onegin* the point of no return comes when Lensky asserts the imagined right to possess a lover, Olga, over whom he jealously and tragically challenges Onegin to the duel in which he himself will die. The reflective and imposing ensemble-chorus (the finale to Act 2 scene 1) which follows that challenge is one of the greatest achievements of nineteenth-century opera. In the coronation scene of *The Maid of Orléans,* Joan of Arc hangs her head in silence after her father confronts her with the question "Do you consider yourself holy and pure?" She has fallen in love with the knight Lionel, and that earthly love, she feels, clouds her divine mission. Her act of assertion is of a different order of magnitude, for it is turned so far inwards upon herself that it passes, numinously, to the universal. She surrenders herself to mortal danger (movingly, even in the fantasized terms of the libretto) for God's and humanity's sake. The ensemble-chorus that succeeds this, opened by the King, to the words "She hung her head" (part of the finale to Act 3), is the underrated highpoint of that score.

When Natalia runs for protection to Morozova, who warns her not to ruin her young life by ignoring her father's wishes, but return home, Tchaikovsky, with considerable dramatic acumen, employs a lyrical melody for Natalia's response: "I will not go to my father's house, I will not throw myself at his feet." That lyricism is a powerful portent of tragedy, for Natalia at this moment exults in the risk she feels she must take by placing upon its head the crown of a beautiful melody. Although it may be seen as an act of foolhardy idealization, it is also, indubitably, a statement of human courage, an ennoblement of the spirit through a proud acceptance of risk. Indeed, Natalia exclaims that she is prepared to die rather than face life without Andrei, whom her father would deny her. The tightening of the screw in *The Oprichnik*— that is, the sequence of events and their musical treatment building up to the monumental ensemble-chorus—is as follows.

Natalia addresses her father when he arrives in a melody that may seem, on the other hand, surprisingly insipid—a tune in twelve-eight time in a similar mold to much salon music for piano by minor nineteenth-century composers. Yet there is a rich ambivalence between the submissive quality of that melody and the terrible nature of the challenge that Natalia here presents Zhemchuzhny with: If he wishes to tear apart the bond between herself and Andrei (to whom she had long since been betrothed) she will renounce him as her father. The weakness of her situation—confronted by her father and his servants, having run to his hated enemy for succor—is portrayed by the feeble tune, whereas her courage is conveyed by the strength of her words and the impassioned way in which she stretches this thin melody to the upper reaches of her vocal range as she exclaims that God defends her. She sings this in F major; the same melody is adopted by Morozova, but in D flat major, as she lends support (in similarly disadvantaged circumstances, faced with Zhemchuzhny and his retainers) by now demanding that Zhemchuzhny atone for his sin and allow Natalia to return to Andrei. She similarly draws the melodic line toward the top of her compass when she declares that the Almighty protects Natalia. After the dramatic arrival of Andrei, Basmanov, and the other oprichniks, which confounds Zhemchuzhny's intention of removing his daughter, Andrei himself then repeats that same melody. His situation is the most dire, weakened in two respects: He is confronted by his mother whom he had earlier, in effect, reassured (in Act 2 scene 1) that he would not consort with Basmanov or join the oprichniks, and he is now among those very oprichniks whom he joined through an oath involving the renunciation of his mother. He accordingly renders the tune (now in E major and six-eight time) in the weakest way of the three occasions on which it appears—he does not actually sing its first phrase (the orchestra presents that instead), but joins it in due course only tentatively, and he is denied the great upward-rising phrase to which Natalia and Morozova had each invoked the name of God. Andrei does not mention the Almighty; his text begins "Whoever I may be now, I love you as before, my own one."

Before Morozova's curse and the ensemble-chorus to which it gives rise, Andrei in vain attempts to placate his mother by stating his irrevocable stand upon principle: He seeks revenge on behalf of his father.

Among the work's several leitmotifs is the theme representing the oprichniks themselves, a grim melody first heard in D minor in the opera's

Prelude. This is by far the work's most frequently used leitmotif, sounding again in Act 1 when Basmanov tells Andrei of the joys of the oprichniks' life, proliferating in Act 2 scene 2 during Andrei's oath-taking, and recurring to great dramatic effect in Act 3, most notably as Morozova renounces her son. The insistence upon the theme gains an obsessive quality during that scene, partly reflecting her anger at Andrei for having joined the oprichniks, but also signifying that in giving in to her own hatred she has become infected with the same evil that motivates the Tsar's thugs. When she sings the curse "Know then, know then: I disown you! Go, oprichnik. Go, Go," the oprichniks' leitmotif is stated four times, each time shifting a half step higher. (It occurs in C minor at first, then is wrenched upwards to appear as C sharp minor; in truncated form it then moves to territory a semitone further up, and, indeed, then a semitone higher still.) The result is that no firm sense of key remains. That creates a disorientating musical environment, one suited to the horror of a mother's renunciation of her son.

Morozova herself is associated with a leitmotif, which first appears in A major in the Prelude, and then in D flat major in Act 2 scene 1 in her duet with Andrei, at her words "Dear son, don't leave me alone to my bitter fate." It specifically conveys the loving dependence she has upon her son. Just before the Prelude's coda the leitmotif is transformed to a very different state, its note-values speeded up and its basic shape stretched out to a great length—as though it needs to insist upon itself as a defence against anxiety. This version of the leitmotif is used very effectively at the opera's conclusion, when Morozova is led in by Viazminsky (whose general ill-intent she senses) to witness her son's execution.

The invariably offstage presence of Ivan the Terrible is represented (when he is alluded to by other characters in Act 4) by a short fanfare-leitmotif, employing (in references to his wishes by Viazminsky) a harmonic quirk based on the passage that comes immediately after the occurrence of the whole-tone scale in Act 1 of *Ruslan and Liudmila* at the heroine's abduction. A group of almost unrelated chords is artificially hung, as it were, on the line of a single, constantly sounding pitch that is common to each. Glinka had used those means to underline Chernomor's magic, which empowers him to prevent the characters onstage from rushing off to rescue Liudmila since the wicked dwarf holds them immobilized. Tchaikovsky uses the device to portray Ivan the Terrible's deviousness, his ability to turn in different directions while apparently remaining constant in intention. The Tsar's seeming resolution of all Andrei's difficulties (by allowing him Natalia against Zhemchuzhny's wishes and permitting him to relinquish his oprichnik's vows) is counterbalanced by the ominous proviso that Andrei is obliged to remain an oprichnik until midnight. The Tsar's command that Natalia be brought to him alone—which Andrei cannot honorably accept, but which his oath of loyalty demands he raise no objection to—precipitates the tragedy.

After Andrei's execution and his mother's death from both the horror of it and the sense of shame in having disowned him, the distant chorus of oprichniks sings their leitmotif, transformed to a major key (A major), exalting the Tsar. Tchaikovsky subtly mitigates the atmosphere of abomination by allowing it to be revealed by the musical tones themselves: The oprichniks' would-be jubilant song lasts a mere eight measures, such a brief taste of jubilation that it reveals that any belief in it as genuine jubilation is only self-deception. Furthermore, the orchestra then presents, in the bass, a melodically enunciated augmented triad, belonging to Chernomor's whole-tone-scale sphere of evil. However much the oprichniks themselves believe in their own evil, the music reassures the audience that deep down all is still right with the world, a testament both to music's power and the perceptiveness Tchaikovsky was slowly acquiring as an operatic dramatist in balancing the respective elements of the work, verbal and musical.

CHAPTER FOUR

UKRAINIAN FOOTWEAR AND A COMIC OPERA: CHEREVICHKI (REVISION OF VAKULA THE SMITH)

UNUSUAL CIRCUMSTANCES GOVERNED the composition of Tchaikovsky's fourth opera and caused a lack of balance. Grand Duchess Elena Pavlovna commissioned Iakov Polonsky to write a libretto based on Gogol's humorous story *Christmas Eve* (from *Evenings on a Farm near Dikanka*) for Alexander Serov, who had barely started to compose his opera when he died in 1871. A competition was then instituted, under the auspices of the Russian Musical Society, for participants to set Polonsky's text for a monetary prize and a production at the Mariinsky Theater. Tchaikovsky entered into discreditable maneuvers regarding the contest. He genuinely mistook the stipulated submission date for the score, believing it to be 13 January instead of 13 August 1875, but, having delivered his work and only then discovering his error, he became impatient to see it staged and made inadvisable enquiries as to withdrawing the opera from the competition and having it produced by the Mariinsky anyway. Despite this and other irregularities, Tchaikovsky gained first prize, the other entries apparently being very far below the level of his. The speed of composition had sharpened his creative faculties, but it also engendered certain flaws, such that he returned to the opera, which he originally entitled *Vakula the Smith*, over a decade later, substantially revising both the music and, almost unaided, the libretto. Tchaikovsky's only help from a literary collaborator was that of Nikolai Chaev, who wrote the text of the hero's interpolated arioso in Act 3, which was requested by the singer Dmitry Usatov, the performer of the revised role of Vakula. The modified version of the opera took its new name, *Cherevichki*, from a kind of Ukrainian footwear that forms the comic crux of Gogol's tale. The story of *Cherevichki* is as follows:

Act 1 scene 1:   Christmas Eve; a street in Dikanka in the Ukraine. The evening. After a scene in which the Devil flirts with the witch Solokha, mother of Vakula the smith, the Devil in a soliloquy sings of his fury at her son for having done a painting of him that is amusing the other devils. He raises a snowstorm to spoil an impending visit of Vakula's to his beloved Oksana by stopping her father, Chub, from leaving home to do some carousing. Even so, Chub ventures out, with his friend Panas, toward the tavern.

Act 1 scene 2:   Chub's cottage. Sad and alone, Oksana admires herself in a mirror. Vakula enters and is dismayed by her vanity. Suddenly she spots him and curtly asks if the trunk he is making for her is ready. It nearly is, but Vakula tells her he just wants to talk with her and look at her. Her cold reply does not prevent him declaring he would prefer her to half the realm. She counters with the alarming declaration that her father will marry Vakula's mother, then withdraws to a partitioned section of the room. Chub appears, covered in snow and unrecognizable. Vakula forces him back into the street. Oksana returns and learns of her father's predicament, scolding the abashed Vakula.

The snowstorm passes. Oksana pretends she loves another young man who, unlike Vakula, is "not an old woman." Despite his hurt feelings, she continues her taunts. She asks him if he really believes that a bumpkin such as he could be loved by such a beauty as she. He leaves, dubbing her a "snake in the grass." Some young folk arrive, but she feels unable to join them in their fun. When they are gone, she admits, in tears, that she loves Vakula.

Act 2 scene 1:   Solokha's cottage. There is further flirtation between the Devil and Solokha. They dance a *Gopak*. After a knock at the door, the Devil hides in a coal sack, afraid it might be the mayor who, if drunk, would make the sign of the cross on himself. Then enter, successively, the mayor, the schoolteacher, and Chub, each showing amorous intent to Solokha (in Chub's case Solokha initiates the flirtation) and each jumping into a sack to hide as the next knock on the door is heard and the next man enters. A fourth knock comes—Vakula's. Chub comically climbs into the same sack as the distressed schoolteacher, who pokes his head out and calls to Solokha. The various heads pop out, the mayor, the school teacher, and Chub each bemoaning their stuffy confines, and the Devil relishing the proceedings. All the heads pop back in as Vakula enters. Although dejected, he keeps himself occupied by clearing the cottage of the sacks. Lovelorn, he is further dismayed at his apparent loss of strength as he tries to lift the sacks. Somehow, he takes them out into the street.

Act 2 scene 2:   Outside in the street, as at the start of the opera. Young
Christmas carol singers appear. Some elderly people come and listen.
Oksana and her friend Odarka arrive in a sleigh. Seeing Vakula with the
sacks, Oksana embarrasses him in front of the crowd by hinting at his
unfortunate expulsion of her father from his own home. She then notices
Odarka's fine *cherevichki* (Ukrainian boots of soft leather), remarking that,
unlike her friend, she has nobody to get her all she needs. Vakula offers to
get cherevichki for her. Oksana announces that if he gets for her the very
same cherevichki that the Tsaritsa wears, she will marry him. After the
youngsters, apart from the dejected Vakula, have a snowball fight, Oksana
teases him so cruelly that the crowd tries to convince him she is only jok-
ing. Vakula exits, carrying only one sack and vowing to put a sinful end to
himself. From the other two sacks, which the chorus unties, jump the
mayor, the schoolteacher, and Chub. The first two retreat from the crowd.
Chub blurts out, "Well, what a wonderful joke I've played on you!" All dis-
solve into laughter.

Act 3 scene 1:   By the river, in moonlight. A distant chorus of lament from
some *rusalki*, imprisoned by the ice on the river, disturbs a wood goblin,
who spots Vakula approaching. Enter Vakula with the sack. He sings a
baleful song, interspersed with echoes from a small, offstage chorus of
male voices. He contemplates drowning himself. When he puts the sack
down, the Devil jumps from it and onto his back, demanding he sign his
name in blood, for by so guaranteeing the Devil his soul, he shall have
Oksana. Pretending to get a nail from his pocket with which to prick himself, Vakula grasps the Devil's tail and pins him to the ground. Acknowl-
edging defeat, the Devil promises Vakula whatever he wishes. Vakula
demands to be taken to the Tsaritsa, and the Devil flies him to St. Petersburg on his back.

Act 3 scene 2:   A reception room in the Palace. The Devil flies in bearing
Vakula and hides as a group of cossacks appears. To get the cossacks to
take him with them to the Tsaritsa, whom they are shortly due to see,
Vakula summons the help of the Devil, who duly fixes in their minds the
idea that Vakula's presence might be useful to them. One of the Tsaritsa's
functionaries appears to escort the cossacks to the Great Hall.

Act 3 scene 3:   The Great Hall. Vakula and the cossacks see a group of
courtiers dance the *Polonaise*. A royal personage [designated as "His Highness," an expedient to avoid problems with the censor whereby the Tsaritsa
could be represented without actually having to appear on stage] appears,
proclaiming that a great military victory has been won. After general jubilation, and His Highness's rendition of a poet's victory ode, the cossacks are
invited to come forward to address the business that brings them here, as a
Minuet is danced in the background. His Highness promises them an
answer to their petition in several days. As he is about to leave, one of the
cossacks prods Vakula, who steps forth with his request for a pair of the

Tsaritsa's cherevichki for his betrothed. His Highness promptly sends for this gift, which is brought in on a silver tray. Vakula is astonished. The entertainments continue, with a *Russian Dance* and a *Cossacks' Dance*. The Devil returns and flies Vakula homewards.

Act 4:   Christmas morning, amidst bright sunshine and a crowd scene at the square in Dikanka. Solokha and Oksana sing a lament at Vakula's disappearance, the former fearing he has taken his own life, the latter smitten with remorse. Oksana believes she has caused his destruction. She exits. The mayor and Panas appear with Chub, who issues a general invitation to the men to a feast at his home, and as they decide whether to go there or to the tavern, Vakula appears, to Solokha's profound relief. Vakula invites Chub to punish him for his misconduct on Christmas Eve. Chub forgives him and agrees to Vakula's request to marry Oksana, who now reappears.

Vakula presents her with the cherevichki, but Oksana declines. Chastened, she no longer needs to demand some mere token of love, but has come to understand love itself. Chub gives his daughter his blessing as Vakula's bride. Players of the kobza (a type of Ukrainian lute) and the assembled company serenade them.

Vakula the Smith, composed in 1874, was first performed at the Mariinsky Theater (St. Petersburg) on 6 December 1876, conducted by Nápravník. *Cherevichki*, which the composer worked on in 1885, was premiered at the Bolshoi Theater (Moscow) on 31 January 1887, conducted by Tchaikovsky himself. By writing *Vakula the Smith* more quickly than was required (he began work in June 1874, completing the opera on 2 September, apart from the Overture, which was finished by 17 October), thereby opening the floodgates to his musical creativity above all else, Tchaikovsky inevitably paid insufficient attention to the dramatic design. He told Mrs. von Meck in November 1878 that in *Vakula* he had been too "forgetful of the *theatrical and visual* requirements of operatic style. The whole opera suffers throughout from the *piling up*, the *excess* of detail, [the] cloying chromaticism in the harmony," adding that there are "lots of tasty titbits in it, but not much simple, healthy food," and even calling its faults "irremediable."[1] However, only a month or so after making that judgment, he embarked on *The Maid of Orléans* (completing the original version in 1879), the first opera in which he turned his attention fully to the dictates of drama, learning almost ruthlessly to curb musical inventiveness for its own sake. Some of the virtually measure-by-measure censorship that one senses in this regard in much of *The Maid* can be seen applied retrospectively in various locations in *Cherevichki*, for in this revision (which dates from three years after some alterations, in 1882, to *The Maid*) Tchaikovsky discarded many of the undue musical complexities of *Vakula the Smith*, replacing them with simplified, leaner textures that better delineate the drama. For example, in *Vakula*, Tchaikovsky had painted an evocative musical picture of Chub and Panas's stumbling around in the Devil's snowstorm in Act 1 scene 1, with chromatic figuration whirling between woodwinds and strings, above a trudging pizzicato bass line, the harmonic structure interspersed with shifts of a tritone (a traditional way of depicting the Devil's influence, as the tritone has been known since the Medieval period as "*diabolus in musica*," i.e., "the Devil in music"). This creatively effective intricacy nevertheless provided much distraction from the vocal parts, and in the definitive version, Act 1 scene 1 of *Cherevichki*, Chub and Panas project their voices more easily above the much simpler texture of a string tremolo; the pizzicato line and most of the chromaticism have been removed.[2] (Unless otherwise stated, all further comparisons between material in *Vakula the Smith* and its counterpart in *Cherevichki* have the same Act and scene designation; precise locations within the scenes are indicated in the footnotes.) Similarly, in the snowball fight in Act 2 scene 2, Tchaikovsky tautologously suggests the participants' physical actions, with a melodic fragment presented in increasingly quicker note values. That elaborate texture is also removed in *Cherevichki*, with a string tremolo introduced instead as support to the lines sung by the chorus and Oksana.[3]

Laroche felt that Tchaikovsky's "main fault [in *Vakula*] (like Wagner in 'Die Meistersinger von Nürnberg') lies in that he has taken the fate and the feelings of his characters too much to heart, so that the music is too warm, too, one might say, tragic for the events, that the lyrical enthusiasm . . . prevents the spectator from laughing at the amusing figures on the stage."[4] That is, at least in its essentials, a fair criticism of Tchaikovsky's opera, for depicting the agonies a lover may endure was a potent aspect of *Vakula the Smith*, however overdone in the putative comic context that was (this work impressively heralding, nonetheless, the full expression of love's torments in his next opera, *Eugene Onegin*). Vakula's anguish as he stands aside during the snowball fight, pondering Oksana's cruelty in testing his love by demanding the Tsaritsa's boots as token of it while she and their young companions have their frolic, is represented with great psychological acumen by the composer. The melodic fragment just mentioned, which is treated to a giddy acceleration, is a reuse of the music from the aria in Act 2 scene 1 in which Vakula had bemoaned the pain his love of Oksana causes him (specifically, the part of the tune which the orchestra had played while the hero had sung, "Passion has destroyed me, I shall fade away").[5] Its quotation and treatment here, therefore, helps us see the snowball fight through the eyes of Vakula's heart, for as his friends and Oksana's snowball fight picks up pace, so his torment increases. Yet Tchaikovsky was right to remove this material in the revised version, for psychological insight in this context is less fitting than the amusing stage picture.

On the other hand, Tchaikovsky was adept at putting the near-tragic to comic use, as in Solokha and Oksana's nicely exaggerated chromatic wailing in Act 3 scene 4 of *Vakula* (Act 4 of *Cherevichki*)[6] prior to the reappearance of

Vakula, presumed deceased although, it turns out, very much alive. (Indeed, in view of that music, Solokha's exclamation when she sees her son carries great point: "What on earth was I thinking of, to go lamenting and howling like an idiot. . . !")[7] Even more notably, Tchaikovsky achieves a comic stroke that perhaps few composers could in rendering Vakula's lines in Act 3 scene 3, once presented with the Tsaritsa's boots: "What adornments!"—such marvels that he feels the feet that wear them are no doubt "of pure sugar!"[8] Here the composer again reuses the melody of the heartfelt aria in which Vakula had lamented his (as he sees it) rejection by Oksana (which had recurred during the snowball fight in the preceding Act). Tchaikovsky now accompanies the melody with mechanistic bursts of rhythm from the strings, enhancing the passionate nature of Vakula's melody with such a shrewd sense of overstatement that he manages simultaneously to portray his hero as the overawed, rural ingenu at the royal court and as a lover riven by anxiety at the very moment of being presented with the supposed key to his desires. A feeling comes across of Vakula having doubts as to whether Oksana will accept both the boots and *him*, as promised.

The reemployed melody from Vakula's Act 2 scene 1 aria may be viewed as the leitmotif of his anguish in love. Fairly little else might be seen as a leitmotif in either *Vakula the Smith* or *Cherevichki*, whereas Rimsky-Korsakov's *Christmas Eve* (1894–95), to a libretto by Rimsky-Korsakov himself on the same Gogol story as that of Tchaikovsky's opera,[9] employs leitmotifs extensively. Rimsky's Vakula is distinguished by a personal leitmotif of a curt, pithy nature, recurring very frequently indeed throughout his opera (unlike the few occurrences of the melody representing Tchaikovsky's hero's amorous distress), emphasizing the smith's steadfastness. The love plot is not strongly expressed in musical terms in Rimsky's work (this being a characteristic flaw of his operas in general, although in *Christmas Eve* he thereby evaded the difficulties which Laroche underlined in Tchaikovsky's setting of the tale).

Vakula the Smith marks the peak of Tchaikovsky's artistic closeness to the Mighty Handful. The correlations in style and outlook are striking. At about the same time that Tchaikovsky began composing *Vakula*, Musorgsky started work on his *Sorochintsy Fair* in the summer of 1874 (leaving it in a sadly incomplete and fragmentary state at his death in 1881), and four years later Rimsky-Korsakov (who had been one of the judges in the competition to which Tchaikovsky had submitted *Vakula*) commenced his *May Night*, both being comic operas based, like Tchaikovsky's, on tales from *Evenings on a Farm near Dikanka*. All three composers employed authentic Ukrainian folk songs in those operas, drawn from Alexander Rubets's collection *216 Ukrainian Folkmelodies* (published in Moscow in 1872), and although Tchaikovsky used much less of this material than his two rivals, he compensated for that by a striking ability to absorb and reproduce the idiosyncrasies of the Ukrainian folk idiom. For example, the opening lines of the opera are sung by

Solokha to an actual Ukrainian folk theme (no. 134 in Rubets's publication). Although expressively quite different in its reflective tone to the vivacious E major *Gopak* (a duple meter Ukrainian dance) that she then performs with the Devil, to a melody that is, it seems, Tchaikovsky's own, there is no incongruity; the scene progresses seamlessly in terms of musical style. Tchaikovsky caught the Ukrainian folk manner just as well in the *Gopak* that Solokha and the Devil dance in Act 2 scene 1.[10] By contrast, the famous *Gopak* from *Sorochintsy Fair* is an authentic Ukrainian folk melody.

The whole-tone scale appears, with its typical supernatural associations, in *Vakula the Smith* during the Devil's snowstorm[11] and in *Sorochintsy Fair* in the intermezzo depicting a witches' sabbath. Although it is remarkable that Rimsky-Korsakov removed that whole-tone scale when, five years after Musorgsky died, he revised his friend's intermezzo as the celebrated concert work *Night on Bald Mountain* (substituting the commonplace chromatic scale), he was, even so, fully receptive to Glinka's scalar innovation. For example, he used the whole-tone scale very forcefully in *May Night* on bass trombone, accompanying a tirade of the village mayor's in Act 2 scene 1 against a youth (unbeknown to him, his own son) who has taunted him in demonic disguise.

As well as the whole-tone scale, two further musical devices employed by Glinka to underline Chernomor's magic powers in his abduction of the heroine in *Ruslan and Liudmila* are to be noted as influences on *Vakula*. One, which we observed adapted as harmonic framework of the Tsar's leitmotif in *The Oprichnik*, is the artificial imposition of unity upon disparate chords by emphasizing a pitch common to each. This features again in the entr'acte preceding Act 3 of *Vakula*[12] and reappears in the interlude at the start of Act 3 of *May Night*, the supernatural context being closely comparable since Tchaikovsky's hero is about to appear in a scene with offstage rusalki, and Rimsky-Korsakov's (namely the aforementioned mayor's son) is about to appear in one with onstage rusalki, nighttime being the setting in both cases. (Rimsky's interlude is actually marked as a depiction of "a Ukrainian night," one of nature's own enchantments.)

Secondly, Glinka included as part of Chernomor's music a series of dissonances—major seconds—none of which resolve, consequently emphasizing the feel of circumvented natural laws. This procedure recurs in the snowstorm in *Vakula*,[13] as it had (although more extensively, indeed with a remarkable sense of determination) in Borodin's songs *The Sleeping Princess* (1867) and *The Sea Princess* (1868).

In no other composition did Tchaikovsky display *Ruslan and Liudmila's* influence more than in *Vakula the Smith*, this being strongly bound up with the general stylistic proximity of *Vakula* to the music of the Mighty Handful, for whom Glinka's second opera was preeminent. Edward Garden observed that Vakula's great aria in Act 2 scene 1 bears a "close relationship"[14] to Liudmila's aria in Act 4 of Glinka's work; that marks a notable fusion of style, for Vakula's melody is, nevertheless, a powerfully Tchaikovskian cantilena.

A surprising, although fairly minimal, influence evident in parts of *Vakula* is the echoing of a style of heightened recitative pioneered by Dargomyzhsky in his radical opera *The Stone Guest* (begun in 1866, still incomplete at the composer's death in 1869, finished by Cui and Rimsky-Korsakov, the latter orchestrating the score). Dargomyzhsky had attempted to convey the inflections of actual spoken Russian in musical terms in that work. Taruskin has drawn attention to a comparable manner in *Vakula,* and he pointed out that Tchaikovsky moved away from this in *Cherevichki* by strategically inserting some new vocal numbers in his more typically melodious vein, "enhancing the predominance of lyric melody over declamatory writing."[15] In view of Tchaikovsky's openly stated loathing of Dargomyzhsky's declamatory style, his obeisance to it in *Vakula* may merely have been a display of keeping up with the times in a work designed for a competition. For whatever reason, his adaptation of the Dargomyzhskian method brought him closer in yet another way to the Mighty Handful, who had shown much excitement at Dargomyzhsky's experiment, with Rimsky-Korsakov emulating it in *The Maid of Pskov* (first version 1868–72, a tale, like Tchaikovsky's *The Oprichnik,* concerning Ivan the Terrible) and Musorgsky in *Boris Godunov.* The latter's astonishingly bold but unfinished *Marriage* (1868) had come much closer to conveying the feel of spoken Russian than had Dargomyzhsky's precedent.

Another new departure in *Vakula the Smith* is the appearance, in Act 3 scene 3, of a *Minuet,*[16] written in late eighteenth-century style, to help portray the elegance of Catherine the Great's court. This is the first occurrence in any of Tchaikovsky's works of his "neo-classical" style, an innocuous portent indeed of the highly atmospheric dramatic usage to which this would be put in *The Queen of Spades.* The minuet in *Vakula* also helps to delineate the boundary between two social worlds, the other being represented by the hectic vivacity of the *Cossacks' Dance.* This was seminal to the contrasts between different strata of society that Tchaikovsky would explore through the medium of dance music in *Eugene Onegin.*

CHAPTER FIVE

PUSHKIN AND THE MATURE OPERATIC BREAKTHROUGH: EUGENE ONEGIN

TCHAIKOVSKY SETTLED UPON Pushkin's "novel in verse" *Eugene Onegin* through good fortune: The opera singer Elizaveta Lavrovskaia suggested it to him, at her home on 25 May 1877, as the source for an opera libretto. He thought the idea "wild" at first, but it quickly fired his imagination. (As it was perhaps Russia's most revered literary text, Tchaikovsky's initial apprehension might be compared to that of an English composer considering the prospect of setting *Hamlet.*) He related to Modest that, after his meeting with Lavrovskaia, he pondered her suggestion during a meal alone at a tavern, then rushed off to buy a copy of Pushkin's text and roughed out a scenario for the opera overnight. The libretto, as finally prepared, was mainly the work of the composer himself, with a limited contribution from Konstantin Shilovsky.[1]

The action, set in Russia in the 1820s, runs as follows:

Act 1 scene 1:   The garden of the Larins' country estate. In this provincial obscurity, two sisters, Tatiana and Olga Larina sing a sentimental, stylized duet about the anguish of love while their mother and nurse chatter to each other about the past. A group of peasants enter with a decorated sheaf to mark the completion of the harvest and sing a folk-style chorus. After a further folk item, a choral dance, Olga sings an aria displaying her girlish, innocent nature, the obverse of her elder sister's romanticized intensity. Olga's betrothed, the poet Vladimir Lensky, arrives bringing with him a friend, the cold and rather cynical Eugene Onegin. A quartet ensues for Tatiana, Olga, Lensky, and Onegin in which Tatiana, out of earshot of Onegin, declares she has fallen in love with him. Lensky then sings a love arioso to Olga.

Act 1 scene 2:   Tatiana's room. That night, sleepless, Tatiana entreats the nurse to tell her about her marriage (which was arranged) but, too distraught to listen, Tatiana suddenly reveals that she is in love. The nurse departs, and Tatiana is left for the rest of the night writing an impassioned declaration of love for Onegin. At dawn, a shepherd is heard playing his pipe; the nurse returns, and Tatiana has her agree to send her grandson to Onegin with the letter.

Act 1 scene 3:   Another part of the garden of the Larins' country estate. Onegin returns to the estate and, in an aria, insensitively but not without dignity, rebuffs Tatiana's avowal of love. The scene is framed at the beginning and the end by an offstage girls' folk chorus.

Act 2 scene 1:   An illuminated ballroom at the Larins' home. A ball is in progress for Tatiana's name day. While dancing with Tatiana, Onegin overhears malicious gossip about him from some elderly ladies. He vows to flirt with Olga so as to gain revenge on Lensky for encouraging him to attend. He leads Olga away, despite Lensky's protests, to dance the *Waltz* with him. Afterwards, Lensky reproaches Olga for ridiculing him and being cruel. She is baffled by his reaction, which in turn makes him more heated; the crucial misunderstanding occurs when Olga protests that Onegin is "very nice!". "Even nice!" replies Lensky, who then accuses Olga of not loving him. He then, suddenly, seeks too immediate a reassurance: He asks Olga to dance the *Cotillion* with him. Onegin cuts in, saying Olga and he had already agreed to dance this together. She declares, "And I'll keep my word!" adding "That's punishment for your jealousy!" The die is cast. A foreign guest, the Frenchman Monsieur Triquet, sings some dainty couplets in honor of Tatiana's name day. Then comes the *Cotillion* (the final dance of a ball, here performed as a mazurka), during which Onegin converses with Lensky and provokes him so much that he openly proclaims Onegin to be no more his friend. The festivities of the assembled company have been interrupted by the argument. Onegin belatedly tries to calm Lensky who is, however, beyond restraint and who challenges him to a duel. An ensemble-chorus follows. Onegin accepts the challenge.

Act 2 scene 2:   Winter, by a rural water mill on the wooded banks of a rivulet, scarcely after sunrise. Awaiting Onegin's arrival for the duel, Lensky sings an aria of nostalgia and fear about his impending fate. Onegin arrives, and they sing a short and extraordinary duet, neither looking at the other, but each voicing to himself regret about the hatred that has parted them, and each unwilling to make amends. Onegin shoots Lensky, then is gripped by horror at his death.

Act 3 scene 1:   One of the side-rooms in a grand mansion in St. Petersburg. A *Polonaise* opens the scene. Onegin then sings of his boredom with all things and of his being haunted by the memory of the friend he killed. Aimless travel has provided no distraction, and he has ended up here. An

Écossaise is followed by the appearance of the Princess Gremina. Her regal bearing astonishes Onegin all the more as she is none other than Tatiana. She has been Prince Gremin's wife for about two years. Gremin sings an aria about how she has restored meaning and youth to his life. The prince introduces them. After a brief conversation in which Tatiana and Onegin both speak of their being previously acquainted, she exits upon grounds of being tired, accompanied by Gremin. Onegin now sings an arioso expressing his love of this transformed Tatiana. He rushes off while around him the *Écossaise* is danced again.

Act 3 scene 2: The drawing room of Prince Gremin's home. Tatiana enters with a letter from Onegin in her hands. His resurgence in her life has disturbed her and stirred latent passions. He enters. She reminds him of the cold lecture with which he repulsed her love for him when she was a girl, and she censures him with pursuing her now because of her social status. Appalled, Onegin vigorously defends the sincerity of his love. Despite all his efforts to win her over, and even though Tatiana is overwhelmed by the force of her own feelings to acknowledge that, indeed, she loves him still, she has, nevertheless, married; Fate has decreed her lot; she will stay true to her spouse. She leaves. Eugene Onegin stands alone, devastated, then flees.

Eugene Onegin, composed from 1877 to 1878, was premiered at the Maly Theater in Moscow on 29 March 1879, conducted by Nikolai Rubinstein. This work marks a turning point in Tchaikovsky's operatic output, away from the overtly nationalist style of *The Voevoda, The Oprichnik,* and *Vakula the Smith.* Folk-based material in *Onegin* is used more sparingly than before, and it now serves, moreover, as a powerful means of articulating the drama at certain crucial junctures. In *The Oprichnik,* we saw how Tchaikovsky briefly explored the dramatic potential of juxtaposing incongruous musical styles: He contrasted some music in comic, Italianate manner—setting Andrei and the oprichniks' action of breaking into Zhemchuzhny's garden—to the mainly Russian folk-inspired quality of the opera in general, in order to depict the manic, dissociated mental state of the hero during his tragically foolhardy action. Pushkin's *Eugene Onegin* gave ample opportunity for such an exploration to be furthered, for it is a highly ironical tale of characters whose lives' emotional orbits make them just narrowly fail to come into genuine contact with each other, and of the mundane or routine social activities of people around them that provide a dissociated backdrop emphasizing the isolation of the individual in the foreground, who strives for happiness but is denied it. One of the poetic novel's most important underlying themes is revealed in the following sentiment, as translated, at any rate, in prose form.

Habit is given to us from above:
It is the substitute for happiness. [2]

Tchaikovsky composed his opera at a point in his life that could hardly have equipped him better to portray the painful non-connecting in Pushkin's characters' lives. Lavrovskaia's suggestion to set *Onegin* came some months after he had reached an appallingly ill-advised decision about his future. In the latter part of 1876, his agonizing over it had led him to decide that he would get married, or enter into some relationship to be displayed openly, with some woman yet to be selected, so as to stop the gossipers' mouths. It was a coldly pragmatic resolution, which apparently took little account of the needs of any future bride, who would merely be a kind of cipher. Although he clearly intended that despite aligning himself with a woman in this way he would not be prevented from continuing a homosexual love life, he was nevertheless aiming to put himself in a strangely contrary position.

While in this topsy-turvy frame of mind, Tchaikovsky composed, and evidently found much release in, the symphonic fantasia *Francesca da Rimini* (October to 17 November 1876), a work of intensely emotional power that marks the break with his early creative period. It is the first full emergence of that expanded emotional range of expression that gave Tchaikovsky his most distinctive, indeed unique, voice. Paradoxically, however, this turning point involved an alien influence, that of Wagner's cycle of four operas, *Der Ring des Nibelungen*, about which Tchaikovsky himself observed to his pupil and friend Sergei Taneyev, "Isn't it odd that I should have submitted to the influence of a work of art that in general is extremely antipathetic to me?" [3] In August 1876 in Bayreuth, he had reviewed the first complete performance of *Der Ring* for *The Russian Register*, and in Paris in January he had seen an opera for which he had far more regard than anything by Wagner: *Carmen*, which had been premiered the previous year, by the French composer Georges Bizet (1838–75). His great love of *Carmen* combined with his loathing of *Der Ring* to produce a remarkable influence upon the Fourth Symphony's festive finale. Garden has pointed out that the forceful recurrence in this movement of the theme representing Fate, which had appeared at the start of the symphony, is "an idea based on the story of the fateful death of Carmen in the middle of the bull-fighting festivities."[4] Brown has suggested that the contours of the symphony's Fate theme may derive from a range of materials in *Der Ring*. Most notably, the descending diatonic scale at the end of Tchaikovsky's theme may relate to the "spear" (also known as the "treaty") leitmotif, the more so as Wagner had "usually blazed [it] forth in lusty brass scoring"[5] on its very frequent appearances.

The ending of Bizet's opera epitomizes the dramatic effect of dissociation, Carmen's murder by her jealous former love Don José, occurring against the background of the crowd being entertained by the bullfight—a personal tragedy juxtaposed with life going on in its usual pattern. Wagner's music represents the edifice, as a Russian musician might have considered it, of Western art-music. It is, therefore, perhaps a particularly dissociative matter that Tchaikovsky's Wagnerian Fate theme should erupt into a Russian folk-influenced symphonic movement, for Tchaikovsky used an actual folk song, "In the field a birch-tree stood" in his finale, observing to Mrs. von Meck, furthermore, that this movement overall represented a "picture of folk celebrating a festival" in the midst of which the individual is not permitted solace in the joys of others for "*Fate* appears again. . . . But the others are oblivious"[6] of him. Moreover, Brown has observed that the apparently Wagnerian influence resulting in the use of a descending scale to embody that ominous force, which would resurge in other representations of Fate (e.g., in *Eugene Onegin* and through to the end of the composer's career), seems "symbolically apt . . . [as] Tchaikovsky saw [Wagner] as the leading assailant upon those values he most cherished."[7]

This extends the artistic line of development observable in *The Oprichnik*, with Italian operatic influence replaced by German and French opera in the dissociative context. The Fourth Symphony's finale was composed concurrently with the significant shift in Tchaikovsky's fortunes caused by the hapless Antonina Miliukova who, be it through fateful or coincidental circumstances, pressed her attentions on him in the wake of his decision in 1876 to marry or enter openly into a relationship with a woman. On 15 May 1877 Tchaikovsky brought to completion the short score (the bulk of the music, apart from the orchestration) of the symphony's first three movements; three days later he received Antonina's third or fourth letter. In this she begged him to meet her and threatened suicide. He first met her on 1 June and shortly thereafter proposed marriage; at roughly this time he finished the short score of the symphony's finale. This movement, Garden has suggested, revealed the composer's "tempestuous emotions"[8] during this astonishing period. Perhaps if those feelings had been any less tempestuous, Tchaikovsky might have lacked that extra, volatile spark of courage needed to commit himself to the task of setting Pushkin's masterpiece. Lavrovskaia's proposal to him of it came exactly halfway between his receipt of his future wife's suicidally daring letter and his scarcely less audacious act of going to meet her. The life-enhancing pivot sat between.

Following Pushkin's lead, the opera employs Russian folk style at certain crucial points in the story, contrasting with art-music, to reflect habit as exemplified in tradition (for folk songs are passed from generation to generation) as distinct from Tatiana's naively romantic hopes of attaining happiness. On the one hand, this background emulation of folk music to some extent defuses the painful predicament in the foreground in which Tatiana finds herself, as common human endeavor will go on regardless of what may happen to her. On the other hand, it underlines the potentially tragic pointlessness of her hopes if she so insists upon them that they dissociate her from more simple aims (those that ordinary folk share).

The emotional core of the opera is the scene of Tatiana's letter to Onegin (part of Act 1 scene 2). In this she movingly sings, to a melody clearly inspired by the Fate motif in *Carmen*, that she entrusts her fate henceforth to him. Though the composer's warmest identification was with his heroine, he also characterized the other main personalities of the opera, Lensky and Onegin himself, with highly perceptive judgment, achieving a more rounded overall pattern of characterization than that of the leading figures in his preceding operas. After the rural Tatiana's sleepless night writing her rash declaration of love to the city sophisticate and general cynic Onegin, whom she had met for the first time only a matter of hours before (he had come to the country upon earlier inheriting his uncle's estate), a shepherd playing a folklike tune on his pipe at the dawn of the next day reaffirms the untroubled world. His highly repetitive melody (a typical folk feature), which contains many statements of a short, three-note unit of rhythm, seems to represent the notion of life as a series of small, apparently insignificant actions, but which can continue easily as they display no great aims. Tatiana interjects, "The shepherd is playing something, everything is peaceful." Another shepherd plays a tune, in answer to the first; Tatiana then exclaims: "But as for me!" Her pensiveness is then impressively conveyed by the orchestra in a brief passage that typifies a trend in late nineteenth-century art-music: It destabilizes the overall sense of key by suggesting several keys in quick succession—and evokes too, no doubt, Tatiana's hopes as too broad to sustain without anxiety. That contrasts markedly with the simple C major world of the first shepherd's melody and the even more tranquil G major of that of the second (constructed over a static, folkish "drone" bass). In Pushkin's original text, a shepherd simply blows on his horn (rather than playing a proper melody on a pipe), awakening the peasants, and to Tatiana "it makes no difference."[9] That degree of dry, ironical detachment typifies Pushkin's novel, whereas the opera's Tatiana actually takes account of the shepherd's playing, and her thoughts in contrasting her internal world with her environment are given extra force by the dynamic immediacy that music can lend the written word. The evolution of Tatiana's character is outlined in detail in the original story, but a composer setting that tale as an opera cannot have the luxury of so many words.[10] In a brief moment here, the operatic setting enables us to glimpse the moral strength of the mature woman latent in the girl—the woman who can so master what she feels for Onegin that when the time would no longer be right for her to have him, when she is married to one of his relatives at the end of the opera, she has the strength to repulse *his* advances toward *her* (much though she still wants him). The seed of this is revealed in the opera by Tatiana recognizing the disparity between the vigilant safeguard constituted by habit—the shepherd's world—and the tumult within herself caused by aiming for an unrealistic happiness. That recognition is the first step in permitting the macrocosm and the microcosm to come

together in the greatest unity that they are allowed. The opera's heroine, perhaps even more than the heroine as Pushkin himself portrayed her, bears out
the truth of the universal sentiment as expressed by Shakespeare:

Love is too young to know what conscience is;
Yet who knows not conscience is born of love?

Immediately after the shepherds' pipings and the music conveying the
heroine's anxious feelings, her nurse enters to awaken (the still awake) Tatiana. The elderly peasant nurse embodies simple folk wisdom, and her arrival
is heralded by her rather folk-tune-like personal leitmotif which, as Brown
points out, is the only melody in the opera "to be associated explicitly with a
particular character (as distinct from a character's emotions)."[11] In that
respect, perhaps the nurse can be seen all the more as representing the
immutable strength of her peasant status for, unlike Tatiana whose imagination has been nurtured by the reading of sentimental novels, the nurse, when
comparably young, could have entertained little aspiration to finding "true
love." Prior to Tatiana writing her letter, the nurse had told her that her own
marriage had been an arranged one. Now she stands like a foil to a kind of
impassioned exuberance displayed by Tatiana, who launches into an A major
melody containing great arches and leaps, as though she has dissociated
herself enough from her anxieties to gain an exhilarating sense of release
from them. To this, she exhorts the nurse to send her grandson to deliver the
note. (Tatiana's lines here, and the nurse's present response, are drawn
directly, with slight variance only, from Pushkin's text.)[12] However, the
ecstatic profile of her melody now expressively falters as she tries to say to
whom the note is to be delivered: "To O . . . to the one who. . . ." For here,
modest, stepwise, scalar movement conveys the melody, broken, as though
through anxiety, by short silences. She then, rather vaguely, reveals that the
intended recipient is "our neighbor"—though the Larins have many neigh-
bors. Understandably puzzled, the nurse replies, "To whom though, my
dear?" and politely adds that her wits are not what they once were. We are
brought down to earth by the nurse's pragmatic reaction as, fittingly, she
sings a melody that emulates one of the most conspicuous features of Russian folk music (strongly emphasizing the ethnic feel that had been
expounded by her leitmotif), descending by step from the fifth step of the
scale to its home tone (in D minor, the key that stands in sober subdominant
minor relation to Tatiana's bright A major). Glinka himself had once called
that type of melodic figure "the soul of Russian music."[13]

At the start of Act 1 scene 3 and again at its close, Pushkin's text for the
song of the servant girls picking berries, which Tchaikovsky sets to a folk-like
tune, is employed to sandwich Onegin's meeting with Tatiana after he has
read her letter. This intensifies the folk music/art-music ambivalence, for as
Tchaikovsky's folk chorus appears twice, it both shows life going on as usual

around Tatiana, prior to Onegin's dashing of her hopes, and life going on around her afterward just as before, however devastated she may now be. In Pushkin's novel the berry pickers' song occurs once only,[14] between Tatiana realizing that Onegin has returned to the Larin estate and his actual appearance before her. When Tchaikovsky's Tatiana rushes in after the end of the first rendition of the berry collectors' chorus, she shatters the folk atmosphere by appearing as the typical, distressed operatic heroine, with the orchestra accompanying her precipitate entry with a series of dissonances (seventh chords) and chromatic coloring.

The reprise of the berry pickers' chorus ends Act 1 and forms the culmination of the repeated shifts between folk-based and Western-oriented style that have given this Act its dynamic and cogent dramatic shape.[15] Although, as we have observed, those juxtapositions all had clear origins, despite adaptation, in Pushkin's text, they all relate back to the archetype of folk style items embodying the concept of habit as life's bulwark: namely, in the opera's opening scene, the two choruses for peasants (the second of which is accompanied by dancing), the text of which does not occur in Pushkin. These choruses, however, are clearly meant to fortify the meaning of Pushkin's great lines (quoted above) about habit being given by Heaven in place of happiness, for just as Tatiana's mother and the nurse finish singing them, the peasants are about to enter bringing the decorated sheaf as token of the harvest's completion. The offstage strains of the first chorus are heard as they approach. This expounds the folk music idiom in distinction to the preceding item, with which the opera begins: Tatiana and Olga's rendition of a sentimental art-music salon duet (sung offstage to an early poem of Pushkin's, *The Singer*,[16] rather than to anything adapted from the novel) which presently mingles with Mme. Larina and the nurse's observations onstage about the past and their deduction that habit is all one may realistically hope for.

At the start of the opening scene of Act 2, Onegin, attending Tatiana's name-day ball, is affronted to overhear malign gossip about him from some of the ladies present and he churlishly determines to upset Lensky in return for his having encouraged him to be here. He waltzes with his friend's adored Olga and conspicuously flirts with her. Olga, subsequently upbraided by Lensky for what he goes so far as to call her cruelty, genuinely does not understand his complaints, and she tries to make him see there is no cause to be offended. Her unwitting trigger phrase, that Onegin is "very nice!", and Lensky's almost comically wounded reply, "Even nice!", are treated by the composer with a perceptive awareness that the oversensitive poet's personality in Lensky must be masterfully represented to make this crucially dramatic scene successful. Olga sings her words in B major and reaches the home tone, B, at the conclusion of her sentence, but the orchestra, as ironic commentator on the situation, does not immediately supply the expected accompanying chord of B, emitting instead a brief flurry of notes and an expressively delayed chord of B. It then wrenches the music toward the remote key of B flat minor, an unsettlingly dark area in comparison to the first key. In this comes Lensky's pained response. There is little hope of true communication, such as might save Lensky from disaster, in view of such a musical rift opening up. The composer had, with a sure touch, conveyed Lensky's vulnerability in his naively overflowing love of Olga in his arioso near the end of the opera's opening scene; there, to a very protracted and therefore artless release of quick notes (continuous eighth-notes filling up the entire space of just over four measures of common time), Lensky had revealed that what he felt for Olga was the love that the soul "of a poet only can love; you alone are in my dreams."

With the exclusivity of Lensky's attachment to Olga now prized apart by Onegin's flirtation, Onegin resurges to hold Olga to her earlier promise for the evening's last dance. Coping with Olga's unkind parting chastisement to let that be a lesson to him, Lensky now experiences Monsieur Triquet singing some verses written in French to honor Tatiana on her name day. To considerable dramatic effect, Triquet's music is a reuse of a tune by the minor, early nineteenth-century composer Amédée de Beauplan, but with new words by Tchaikovsky's co-librettist, Shilovsky (who also helped finalize the shape of the opera's scenario, apart from which it seems the bulk of the libretto was put together by Tchaikovsky himself). As a reflection, in the external world, of Lensky's inner turbulence, the stylistic divisions between Triquet's song, its sweet Gallic charms and early nineteenth-century manner setting it so much apart from the richness of Tchaikovsky's own musical style in the rest of this scene, are deeply effective. Triquet's song may seem like an accessible island of calm. To Lensky, however, in his present emotional predicament, it would surely seem an unreachable, and therefore ironically irrelevant, refuge. The starting point is again in Pushkin's original story, where we are told that Triquet has appropriated his text, with minimal alteration, from "ancient airs in an almanac."[17] When Pushkin's Triquet presently sings, he does so "out of tune"[18]—to Tatiana's, rather than Lensky's, discomfiture. (Onegin's flirtation with Olga has not yet occurred; the off-key singing metaphorically emphasizes Tatiana's sense of alienation, as Lensky, and Onegin—whose embarrassing rejection of her declaration of love is still fresh in her mind—have been placed immediately opposite her upon arriving at the banquet that precedes the ball.)[19]

When matters come to a head in the opera during the last dance at the Larins' ball, and Lensky, furious at Onegin for trying (he believes) to cause Olga's ruin, challenges his former friend to a duel, that summons is immediately followed by a forceful, lengthy, descending scale from the orchestra, echoing the "Fate-scale" in the Fourth Symphony and, as indicated above, the work of Wagner.

Lensky shortly initiates the great ensemble-chorus that brings Act 2 scene 1 to its close. He sings poignantly of the idyllic childhood and the blossoming of love that he had experienced at his beloved's home. But, now, he has realized that "life is no novel." A complex texture develops, Onegin's and Tatiana's voices interweaving contrapuntally with Lensky's. Suddenly, the texture becomes firmer, for the solo voices, for a second, cease. As the chorus makes its first contribution to this finale, all the choral parts align in the same rhythm to proclaim "Poor Lensky!" The subtly suppressive complexity of design of the soloists' preceding music is all the more propulsively succeeded by the chorus's rhythmically united declaration which brings with it a powerful shift of key, to B major, a much sharper and brighter tonal region than the G major tonic of this number's opening.[20] The emphasis on B major is apt, for now that Lensky is beyond the point of no return, the use of the same key for the chorus's commiseration as that in which Olga had previously attempted to dissuade him, to no avail, from jealousy over Onegin's attentions is an irony worthy of Pushkin himself. However, there is no apparent root for it in the novel. Pushkin's Olga does not even seem to notice her lover's jealousy, as, indeed, the author does not write of any argument at the Larins' ball, either between Lensky and Olga, or, indeed, Lensky and Onegin. Lensky has bitter thoughts about what he feels is Olga's coquetry, but these come to him apparently unspoken after Olga unwittingly compounds the effect of Eugene's flirtation with her by denying Lensky the evening's last dance because it is already promised to Onegin. The novel's Lensky saves up his anger to be issued in the form of a note, delivered the next morning, challenging Onegin to the duel.

After Lensky's death in the duel in Act 2 scene 2 and Onegin's subsequent, purposeless travels, he returns, in Act 3 scene 1, to a more sophisticated setting than that of the Larins' ball in the country, for now he finds himself at a high society function in St. Petersburg. Instead of a rather gauche waltz (like that in which Onegin had so tragically ventured to provoke his friend) a majestic *Polonaise* distinguishes the scene. When Tatiana eventually appears, now the wife of Prince Gremin (an unnamed prince in Pushkin's text) her own majestic bearing exemplifies the scene that has been set.

Although formerly indifferent to her, Onegin is now inflamed with love.

From this point in the opera to its end, Tchaikovsky had to confront a potentially acute problem in how to characterize Onegin. Onegin's rival henceforth is not so much Gremin as Tchaikovsky himself, for the composer had provided Tatiana with music of such sweep and lyrical potency in the letter scene that to try to portray the power of love so convincingly twice in the same opera would be to undermine the first achievement. During the letter scene, to a ravishing theme in D flat major, based, deceptively, on a simple descending scale depicting Fate, Tatiana had sung, "Who are you: my guardian angel, or a perfidious tempter?" In the opera's closing stages, Onegin shows himself to be neither, but just an erring man, one who cannot see that it is precisely what he loves in Tatiana that prevents her accepting his advances. Her fruition into a woman of genuine majesty (her elevation in social status through marriage merely confirms in symbolic terms what is in her soul anyway) is the counterbalance to all in Onegin's character that is empty, detached, and bored with the world. She could have been his redemptive wife in other circumstances, but her dignity obliges her to stay true to her husband. Just as it would have been a mistake to provide Gremin with a great love-melody (the modest, though sincere, musical expression of love that he is allocated enhances the dutiful nature of Tatiana's attachment to him), Onegin likewise gets none. The lioness's share of the good tunes go to Tatiana. The only occasion, arguably, in Act 3 in which Onegin is allowed a lyrical incident of any strength is when, in the arioso near the close of its first scene, he declares, "Alas, there's no doubt, I'm in love . . . like a boy," which is sung to the same ecstatic melody to which Tatiana, at the start of the letter scene, had exclaimed of her desire to win Onegin: "Let me perish, but first I shall call up, in dazzling hope, some unknown bliss." But such an undefined and unlikely bliss could not have been summoned, even with Tatiana's dazzling hope, for she was not yet the mature woman who could capture Onegin's then-elusive heart; nor can the mere love stricken youth that has for so long lain dormant in the cynical Onegin now hope for something even more unlikely. The reuse of this striking melody, which necessarily diminishes its impact as a melody per se, is not just a fitting irony, but also a dramatic masterstroke. It portends the diminishing, to the point of disappearance, of Onegin's hope when Tatiana presently rejects him.

The richness of lyrical invention that is so much the heroine's province in this opera is perhaps in large measure the composer's repayment of an unconsciously guilty sense of debt to Antonina Miliukova, a projective enrichment of an operatic character palliating Tchaikovsky's regrettable actions in encouraging the feelings of, and eventually marrying, a woman whom he at no time intended he would treat fully as a wife. Most of *Eugene Onegin* had been written by the time of the wedding, which occurred on 18 July 1877, and its composition began, as we saw, after Antonina's amorous, epistolary advances to Tchaikovsky. Significantly, the first scene he composed of the opera was the one featuring Tatiana's letter to Eugene (i.e., the second scene of Act 1), which he finished sketching after proposing marriage. If, indeed, Antonina inspired Tchaikovsky through the route of his unconscious mind (however remote and unlikely a figure she would have been to do so at the conscious level) then musical history owes her a debt of gratitude for making the composer dragoon the force of his unconscious creativity into erecting such a reparative monument to her as this operatic masterpiece.

Matching the lyricism of the D flat major melody, mentioned above, in Tatiana's letter scene, are two other themes associated with her, in the same key: The first occurs in the opening scene of Act 3, on a solo clarinet, when we first see her as a princess, and the other appears in the following final scene of the opera. To the latter theme she sings to Onegin that in his heart are both pride and true honor—this prior to dropping all pretense as she confesses she still loves the wretched man. All he can then do is utter a few disjointed phrases, with just the faintest echoing of the melodic contour of his beloved's statement about pride and honor; he strives to emphasize his astonished joy, but then enters into fantasy as he exclaims she has returned to being the Tatiana of former times. While he sings of his pleasurable astonishment, the orchestra takes up her great melody, but now in D major, the remotely related key into which the force of her honesty has propelled the music. That wrench upwards by a half-step relates movingly back to the reverse kind of key-shift used to represent the disparity between Olga's B major music and Lensky's B flat minor response during their confrontation in Act 2 scene 1. Lensky's present fate had been to meet his death; Onegin's is to glimpse bliss only to be denied it. When Tatiana says no to him, he is, no less than the Onegin of Pushkin's novel, "as if thunderstricken."[21]

REVERSION TO CHILDHOOD AND AN EFFLORESCENCE OF THE GRAND: THE MAID OF ORLÉANS

TCHAIKOVSKY WAS ATTRACTED to the theme of his next opera, *The Maid of Orléans*, on Joan of Arc—about whom he had once written a poem, as a boy of seven—by reading Zhukovsky's Russian translation of Schiller's play *Die Jungfrau von Orleans*, in the regressive and recuperative aftermath of the collapse of his marriage. That reading presently bore fruit, for in a state of anxiety mixed with excitement, he started writing the work on 17 December 1878 in Florence, Italy, at the point of the scene (in Act 2) of Joan's divinely sanctioned recognition of the French king, who is posing as someone else, deliberately to test if God is empowering her. Tchaikovsky was the sole librettist for this opera, and in addition to Zhukovsky's translation of Schiller's text, he eventually used four more sources for the libretto, all in French, and all simply entitled *Jeanne d'Arc*: the opera by Auguste Mermet (1810–89) of which it seems he had a copy of the vocal score, rather than just the libretto;[1] the play by Jules Barbier;[2] and the biographical-historical studies by Jules Michelet and Henri Wallon. The plot of Tchaikovsky's opera, set in early fifteenth-century France, which he devised with great labor from his sources, is as follows:

> Act 1: A rural setting; on the right, a chapel with an icon of the Holy Mother, and on the left a tall, broadly spreading oak on the bank of a stream. A chorus of girls adorns the oak tree with garlands. Joan of Arc, her father Thibaut, and her intended husband, Raimond, enter. As the English overwhelm France, Thibaut wishes Joan the security of being married, but she states her destiny is preordained. He tells her she is acting at the Devil's behest. Why does she love to linger at the oak, a haunt of evil? He warns of God's vengeance.

Fleeing the enemy, a group of peasants enter, one of whom, Bertrand, relates that Orléans is under siege. Aiding the English are the treacherous duke of Burgundy and Queen Isabella—none other than the mother of the French king. Bertrand hopes the English commander, Salisbury, will perish. Joan declares that an armed maid will raise the siege. Thibaut tries to silence her, but she exclaims that Salisbury is already dead. A soldier appears, with news that Salisbury has indeed been killed. Thibaut leaves, disturbed by Joan's vision. Joan initiates a choral hymn. All exit except her. She sings a farewell aria to the countryside that saw her raised. She feels that her time has come, but exhorts God to let her continue her humble way of life. An offstage chorus of angels tell her to don warrior's armor, forgo earthly love, and lead the king to Reims to be crowned. She pledges herself to her mission.

Act 2:   A hall in the Palace of Chinon. The king, the future Charles VII, tries to take refuge in entertainments and the love of his mistress, Agnès, as France disintegrates. The knight Dunois chides him for wishing lavishly to reward the gypsies, pages, dwarfs, jesters, and skomorokhi (wandering minstrel-clowns) who have just danced for him, when the treasury has no money to pay the army, who threaten to desert. Agnès exits. A wounded soldier, Loré,[3] enters and relates another defeat; the king must escape, or grasp hope now and go to his troops. Loré dies. Crushed, and lamenting the loss of life, the king would retreat. Declaring "We have no king!" Dunois leaves, intending to die honorably at Orléans. Agnès returns, promising her wealth for the king's cause. Nevertheless he despairs. She consoles him in an arioso, and they sing a short love duet.

The tide turns. Dunois reappears with a crowd and news of a great victory. A "savior-maid" has arisen. An archbishop appears, confirming to the astounded Charles that a maid had miraculously rallied his soldiers and defeated the enemy. She states that she is a prophetess and vows to raise the siege of Orléans.

After an excited flurry at Joan's imminent arrival, Charles decides to test her, telling Dunois to act as though *he* were king. Joan appears, with others. She picks out the true king although she has never set eyes on him before, tells him God guides her, and describes the contents of two prayers that he had said to the Almighty. Convinced, he prevents her relating a third. At the archbishop's invitation, Joan tells them all of her humble background as a shepherd's daughter in Domrémy. The Virgin Mary had come to her as she prayed at the oak, saying she had been chosen to set France free, and crown the king.

In the finale to the Act, all sing their recognition of Joan's divine mission. The king grants her control of the army. She asks for the archbishop's blessing. All urge her to lead France to victory.

Act 3 scene 1:   Close to the battlefield, with the English camp burning in the distance. A knight, Lionel, appears, followed by Joan who, learning that he is of the treacherous Burgundian faction, attacks and defeats him. But as she prepares to kill him, a moonbeam lights up his face: she somehow cannot proceed. She makes a sign to him to escape. This he will not do. She then tells him to kill her and go. He is amazed; she lifts her sword again, but again cannot use it. She exclaims, "Holy Virgin!" He begins to fall in love with her. He takes her by the hand, Dunois approaches from offstage, and Joan again tells Lionel to go, but he declares his love for her. Dunois enters and Lionel offers him his sword; Dunois accepts that he thus returns to the king's side, gives back the sword, and then informs Joan of the enemy's defeat and of the opening up of the gates of Reims. Joan falls exhausted into Lionel's arms. She has a wound, and she wishes her flowing blood would take her life away with it.

Act 3 scene 2:   The square at Reims Cathedral. A majestic coronation procession passes into the cathedral. Thibaut and Raimond remain behind. Raimond tries to persuade Thibaut to depart, but he has witnessed his daughter's distraught features and feels it his duty to save her soul, at whatever cost. The king, Joan, and the rest of the procession come forth from the cathedral. The king thanks Joan, and extends this to pledging that an altar be built to revere her, and begs that she reveal her "immortal image" so that they may worship her. Joan says nothing but lets out a cry as Thibaut steps into view. He condemns her as an instrument of the Devil, to which the crowd reply that he is mad. He states that it is they who are mad. Then he asks Joan, "In the name of the Trinity, do you consider yourself holy and pure?" She is again silent; her sense of shame at her love for Lionel prevents her speaking. The crowd is overawed. "She hung her head," sings the incredulous king, initiating an ensemble-chorus concluding with an entreaty to God to reveal the truth. Three claps of thunder ensue, coming respectively after Dunois's challenge to any present who dare accuse Joan, Thibaut's further accusation of her, and the challenging of her by the archbishop. All disperse in anger or bewilderment, but Joan remains, to be approached by Lionel. She denounces him as the destroyer of her soul.

Act 4 scene 1:   A forest. Joan alone; she now cries out for Lionel. He appears and they sing a passionate love-duet. The offstage angels sing again, now accusing Joan of betraying her heavenly mission. She relinquishes Lionel's embrace. English soldiers appear and mortally wound Lionel in his attempt to protect her. She kisses him for the last time, assuring him they will soon be reunited, then is removed by her captors.

Act 4 scene 2:   A square in Rouen. Joan is brought to the stake and is denounced as a witch by the crowd. She asks for a cross, and a soldier breaks a stick in two and fastens the pieces together. A priest holds this crucifix in front of Joan and blesses her as the flames grow stronger. She goes to meet God with an expression of joy lighting up her face.

The Maid of Orléans, composed from 1878 to 1879, was first performed at the Mariinsky Theater on 25 February 1881, conducted by Nápravník (Tchaikovsky revised it the following year). It displays a very considerable simplification of style as compared with *Eugene Onegin*, which, in addition to the choice of the celebrated Western historical figure of Joan of Arc (as opposed to the national one of Ivan the Terrible in *The Oprichnik*, the grand-opera precursor among Tchaikovsky's own operas for this work), points to the composer's wish for public success beyond Russia's borders. Indeed *The Maid* was the first of his operas to be performed abroad, being given in a Czech translation by V. Novotny in Prague on 28 July 1882.

The opera's spectacular coronation crowd scene and the high drama of Joan being denounced by her own father, who aims to vitiate her sins and save her soul, in front of that same crowd and the newly crowned king (whose position as monarch could not have been secured without Joan's efforts) form an impressive stage-picture (Act 3 scene 2), in the full tradition of Meyerbeerian French grand opera. So too, at the opposite extreme of expressiveness, does the extensive ballet section (beginning with the *Dance of the Gypsies*) at the start of Act 2, whose very decorativeness performs the dramatic function of underlining the fecklessness and lack of courage of the king, lost in the frivolity of entertainments while his kingdom collapses, prior to the advent of hope with Joan's arrival. Yet *The Maid of Orléans* failed both at home and abroad. In the former case this was partly just bad luck, as the resounding success that greeted the opera when it opened was followed by the assassination of the Tsar, Alexander II, two weeks later, and the cancellation of the opera season. However, *The Maid* fell from the repertoire after the 1882–83 revival, and Tchaikovsky never saw it performed in his homeland again. The debut in Prague also amounted to little, as the performances there soon ceased.[4]

Although Joan is as much the focal point of the composer's attention in this opera as Tatiana had been in *Onegin*, she is arguably not accorded any melody as beautiful as those provided for the earlier heroine. Yet that, far from being a failing of *The Maid of Orléans*, is one of its great strengths. Tchaikovsky seems to have conceived enough historical regard for the figure of Joan of Arc, despite all the operatic distortions of the libretto, to realize that the basic anomaly she represents—of a girl who saves her nation at God's behest, yet suffers a brutal death—could not be conveyed by appropriating her, as it were, to his own style. There is something fittingly submissive, like an act of self-sacrifice, in Tchaikovsky's subsuming most of his unique melodic powers beneath a musical style in this opera that is (with few moments of exception) remarkably cosmopolitan. Joan of Arc is of the world: She is not exclusively his.

The French style is appropriately predominant, Meyerbeer's G flat major love-duet *"Tu l'as dit"* from *Les Huguenots* again having an influence (as it had on Natalia's arioso in Act 1 of *The Oprichnik*) on the melody of the brief duet for the king and Agnès, in the same key, in Act 2 of *The Maid of Orléans*. The arioso that immediately precedes this, for Agnès, who attempts to console the king as the enemy forces increasingly gain control of his realm, was felt by Abraham to be redolent of Charles Gounod (1818–93), whose opera *Faust*, premiered in 1859, Tchaikovsky greatly admired. Abraham also mentions the operas of Jules Massenet (1842–1912) as generally influencing the lyrical content of *The Maid*. At the other extreme from that particular kind of melodiousness is the overcharged, jaunty angularity of the *Dance of the Jesters and Skomorokhi*, no. 11 (c), in Act 2 of Tchaikovsky's opera, which emphasizes through its excess the king's neglect of his nation's needs while he listens to it. It was derived from the concluding measures of the orchestral introduction to the similarly positioned *Chœur des ménestrels*, no.10, in Act 2 of Mermet's *Jeanne d'Arc*,[5] the failure of which work, premiered in 1876, twelve years after Meyerbeer's death, has been viewed as confirming the end of the Meyerbeerian grand-opera manner's domination in France.

Against this broadly French expanse of style, other Western influences occasionally arise. Indeed, two of the most famous works of European musical culture—one Austrian and one Polish—seem to have been unwittingly recalled by Tchaikovsky in his general concern to look westward in *The Maid*. Abraham noted the recall of the start of the *Jupiter* Symphony by Mozart (1756–91) in the king's music in Act 2 (the opening of no. 13, the item that concludes with the love-duet), and Brown has pointed out the recollection of the A major *Polonaise* for piano by Fryderyk Chopin (1810–49) in Joan's farewell aria in Act 1. Russian influences are dimly perceptible on occasion, but are notable precisely for their rarity (the faintly Glinkan quality of the opera's opening girls' chorus is an illustration).

Tchaikovsky reserves his most conspicuous moment of genuinely Tchaikovskian melody for the terrible turning point in Joan's fortunes. In doing so, he can extend the warmth of sympathy that his lyricism represents without any risk of engulfment. The type of melody he employed on this occasion, in which dignified, scalar motion is interspersed with strongly profiled leaps, would reach the height of its development in the "Rose Adagio" from the ballet *The Sleeping Beauty* and in the great theme for cellos in the *pas de deux* in Act 2 of *The Nutcracker*. There is, indeed, a somewhat dance-like character to the B major melody of the ensemble-chorus in the finale of Act 3 scene 2 following Joan's denunciation by her father. Schiller invented a means of sullying Joan's divine purpose by making her fall in love, with an Englishman, Lionel, whom Tchaikovsky transforms into a Burgundian. When in the opera all are confronted with the astonishing situation of Joan, France's savior, remaining silent at her father's questioning of her state of innocence, that sense of impasse is symbolically loosened by the subtly dancing lilt of the ensemble-chorus's melody. The singers' plea to God to reveal the truth is thus not subjected to any incongruity or banality—which such a musical gesture, unless properly judged, could so easily have been. It is, instead, an affirmation of hope.

Although *The Maid of Orléans* lacks the symphonically organized ingenuity of design of the not-stereotypically-operatic *Eugene Onegin* (a result the composer deliberately sought), and its sweeping rhetoric, accumulated throughout its great length, makes it seem an attempt to out-Meyerbeer the late Meyerbeer at a time when the grand manner in its French home at least was thought passé, it remains in terms of sheer stage impact a work not quite challenged by any of Tchaikovsky's other operas. Perhaps only the tragic ballet *Swan Lake* has a dramatic forcefulness that is comparable to the cathartic sense of tragedy at the end of this most sadly neglected opera.

CHAPTER SEVEN

RETURN TO PUSHKIN: MAZEPPA

TCHAIKOVSKY WROTE *MAZEPPA* to a libretto by the poet Viktor Burenin (which the composer himself modified), based on Pushkin's narrative poem *Poltava.* The director of the St. Petersburg Conservatoire, the cellist and composer Karl Davydov, had originally been intended to write the music, but lacking the necessary time, readily agreed to pass the libretto on when Tchaikovsky, who had heard of his difficulties, approached him for it. Pushkin's poem culminates in an account of Tsar Peter the Great's victory in the battle of Poltava (1709) over the Swedish king, Charles XII, whose invasion of the Ukraine the Ukrainian hetman Ivan Mazeppa had treacherously supported in a bid to oust the Tsar. The opera's main focus, however, is upon the love-intrigue between Mazeppa and his own goddaughter, and all the appalling ravages it causes. The libretto runs as follows:

Act 1 scene 1: Kochubei's garden by the River Dnieper. A chorus of girls tell their fortunes by casting garlands into the river. Peter the Great's main magistrate for the Poltava region, Kochubei, entertains the hetman (cossack chief), Mazeppa. Kochubei's daughter, Maria, feels Fate has decreed her surprising love of the elderly Mazeppa. A young cossack, Andrei, enters and declares his love for Maria, which she does not reciprocate. She blames herself for unintentionally misleading him. Disconsolate, he exits. She enters the house.

Kochubei, his wife Liubov, Maria, Mazeppa and their other guests, emerge from the house onto a terrace. After a *Gopak* is danced in Mazeppa's honor, Mazeppa, to Kochubei's astonishment, asks him for Maria's hand in marriage. He dismisses Kochubei's objections: the age gap and the fact that he is Maria's godfather, which he dubs a "trifling matter," regarding which he will ask for the church's dispensation. Asked by Kochubei, he confirms that Maria loves him and has agreed to marry. Nevertheless, Kochubei forbids the union. As the argument develops, Kochubei declares his friendship with Mazeppa ended and orders him to leave. Mazeppa retorts he has forgotten whom he is addressing. Andrei enters. When Mazeppa calls his guards to arms and Kochubei calls on his servants and guests to show defiance, Maria throws herself between her father and the hetman, begging that the quarrel stop. However, Mazeppa summons another contingent of guards and tells Kochubei that Maria must be allowed to choose freely whether to come with him or part forever from him. After a moment of anguished indecision, she cries out that she is his. He takes her off with him. Liubov runs after her, but faints.

Act 1 scene 2:   A room in Kochubei's house. Liubov and a women's chorus sing a lament about the daughter who has given herself over to Mazeppa's clutches. Kochubei swears Andrei and Iskra to secrecy, then reveals he believes Mazeppa plans a treacherous alliance with the Swedes, against Peter the Great. Kochubei intends to expose this to the Tsar, and Iskra feels the denunciation cannot fail. Andrei, consumed by a need for revenge over Maria's fate, personally undertakes the grave risk of trying to overcome the Tsar's bias toward the hetman and persuade him of his duplicity. Kochubei too vows to live for vengeance's sake alone. A chorus condemning Mazeppa ends the scene.

Act 2 scene 1:   A dungeon in the palace at Belaia Tserkov. Kochubei and Iskra are Mazeppa's captives, awaiting execution the next day. The hetman had presented the Tsar with a slander of them, and the Tsar himself had handed them over to the slanderer. Mazeppa's henchman Orlik enters. Kochubei had previously been tortured into a false confession of guilt. Now he is told to reveal the location of his treasure; he steadfastly refuses. Orlik summons the torturers.

Act 2 scene 2: A room in Mazeppa's palace. Mazeppa eulogizes the beauties of the Ukrainian night sky but, troubled, he sees the stars as "accusing eyes." Kochubei and Iskra must die, he observes. He becomes increasingly ruthless as his political goal nears. Nevertheless, he is concerned at what effect news of their fate will have on Maria. Orlik enters, informing Mazeppa that Kochubei still divulges nothing. Impatient, the hetman orders him to go and prepare the execution for the morning.

Thinking of the terrible blow he is preparing for Maria, he then focuses on his love for her, which in an arioso (interpolated into the opera, to text by V. Kandaurov, at the request of Bogomir Korsov, who created the title role) he describes as a renewal of him in his old age. Maria enters. With appalling and unwitting irony, she states "It's torture" not to see him for a whole day. He pleads matters of government have absorbed his time. She presses her complaint and reminds him she has forsaken everything for him, but his time is all spent with military officers now. She accuses him of interest in another woman. He does not reply directly to that, but unveils his political machinations. He plans to rise up against the Tsar, to make the Ukraine independent, and perhaps become its monarch. Enraptured,

Maria vows to support him, even if they must face their death in the coming conflict. He asks if either he or her father had to die, whom would she choose? Disturbed by this question, she eventually says, "You decide," but adds she is "ready to sacrifice all for you!" The hetman entreats her to remember her words, and he departs.

Maria too now beholds the night's beauty and has forebodings—can she hear her parents' plaints, alone in old age? Liubov appears. At great risk, she is here to implore Maria to prevent her father's execution, due today. Liubov fears Maria's astonishment is feigned, but then sees it is not, and tells her what Mazeppa has clearly kept from her about Kochubei's fate. Maria faints, blaming herself for her father's position. As she bends down to help her daughter, Liubov hears march music in the distance; the troops are bringing Kochubei to be executed. She struggles to rouse Maria, who comes to in a haze. "They're taking your father to execution! Save him!" cries Liubov. They rush out in fearful determination.

Act 2 scene 3:   A field in which a scaffold with two beheading blocks stands behind a rampart. A crowd awaits the victims' arrival, and tries to silence a drunken cossack who strikes up with a ditty about a flirtatious wench. He is indifferent to landowners' heads being chopped off. As the crowd at last pushes him away, two executioners arrive, leading the execution cortege. Mazeppa passes through, disappearing behind the scenes. Kochubei and Iskra are led in and sing a final prayer of repentance to the Almighty, echoed by the crowd. Maria and Liubov rush in just as the axes are raised above the victims. The axes swing down. Maria falls into her mother's arms as the crowd roars in horror.

Act 3:   Kochubei's estate, overgrown, with the terrace half-ruined; nighttime. After an orchestral interlude depicting the Tsar's victory at the battle of Poltava over the Swedish forces—with whom Mazeppa had allied himself—Swedish soldiers are pursued by Russian soldiers across the stage. Andrei enters, hoping here to recapture memories of Maria. Mazeppa appears with Orlik, who leads their horses away. Andrei emerges into view and confronts Mazeppa over the destruction he has wrought upon Maria and her former home. The hetman asks what he wants of him. His death, he replies. Mazeppa is loath to fight, but warns Andrei that he is not unarmed. Andrei rushes at him with a saber, but Mazeppa shoots him. Andrei collapses. The hetman exclaims he did not wish Andrei's ruin. He then goes to look for Orlik—but finds Maria. She has become insane. Although he is appalled by this, his attention must now turn to his own needs, for Orlik returns and warns that others are coming. Dismissing Mazeppa's idea of taking Maria with them as itself mad, Orlik pulls him away and they depart.

Maria notices Andrei. She thinks at first that his bloody form is that of her executed father. Then she declares it is a child sleeping in the grass and, taking Andrei's head in her lap, begins a lullaby. He regains consciousness, and she recognizes his voice as one that sang to her when she was a child. Andrei is unable to bring her mind back to the present situation. He says farewell and dies. She rocks his corpse to the sound of her lullaby, staring fixedly ahead.

Mazeppa, composed from 1881 to 1883, was premiered at the Bolshoi Theater on 15 February 1884, conducted by Ippolit Altani. Tchaikovsky had passed through a phase of disenchantment with his work on it. Having begun composition in the summer of 1881, he temporarily abandoned the opera and turned to Shakespeare's *Romeo and Juliet*, briefly, but abortively, committing himself to setting in operatic form the subject that he had already conveyed in purely orchestral terms in the fantasy-overture of that title (1869, whose second, and definitive, revision had been carried out in 1880, roughly a year prior to commencing *Mazeppa*). He then diverted his attention to a play by Luka Antropov, *Vanka the Steward*, as a possible source for an opera. When he presently came back to the Pushkin libretto, toward the end of 1881, he did so with renewed vigor. He found the impetus to recommence composition by setting the love scene between Mazeppa and Maria (in Act 2 scene 2), in which she is jealous of the amount of time he is spending with his military officers and, she fears, another woman, and he rewards her ambivalent love (or perhaps deflects attention from some amorous infidelity) by suddenly revealing his plans to free the Ukraine of Russian rule, and perhaps become its monarch.

Mazeppa combines elements of the French grand-opera format that had been explored in *The Oprichnik*, and thoroughly embraced in *The Maid of Orléans*, with a strong resurgence of Russian folk style, after its more economical and dramatically focused use in *Eugene Onegin* and its reduction to an extremely slight level in *The Maid*. All three Acts of *Mazeppa* display folk-influence, and the composer showed no less skill in writing themes of his own invention, in the folk manner, than he had in *The Voevoda*, juxtaposing these with authentic folk melodies as seamlessly as he had in his first opera. A particularly attractive folk-like theme, apparently of Tchaikovsky's own devising, appears on the cor anglais, in F sharp minor, in the Overture to *Mazeppa*.

Among *Mazeppa*'s weaker facets is the music written for Andrei which, although highly dramatically effective in the final scene with Maria, seldom rises elsewhere above a basically functional level of inspiration. But as Andrei's role was introduced, as Taruskin has pointed out, to satisfy operatic convention by having a love-plot (here it is just a nominal one) between a tenor and a soprano, the perfunctory nature of his melodic lines is not surprising. Andrei's relationship with Maria, doomed, simply, as she does not reciprocate his love, contrasts with the mutual love between her and the elderly, cruel hetman, whose gravitas is conveyed by the setting of his voice at a lower pitch than tenor, that is, baritone. The opera's first crowd scene (in Act 1 scene 1) in which the supporters of Maria's father, Kochubei, and those of Mazeppa augment the volume of sound (and, theoretically, the stage effect) of the argument between the two men, as the former attempts to forbid the marriage between his daughter and the hetman, is merely dutifully written, and lacks true impact.

Nevertheless, the opera's strengths well outweigh its weaknesses. The grand-opera effect of a genuinely imposing crowd scene is secured in the context of the execution of Kochubei and his associate Iskra (the finale of Act 2 scene 3), who have suffered the appalling fate of being handed over by the Tsar to the man whose aim to drive that same Tsar from the Ukraine they had attempted to expose. Kochubei had subsequently undergone torture in Mazeppa's dungeon in a moving scene (Act 2 scene 1). The impending arrival of the victims at the place of execution, accompanied by the somber strains of an offstage march played by the approaching procession's band (that is, a band used as an extra resource independently of the orchestra) clashes well with an ironical situation onstage. The crowd that has gathered for the beheading is just succeeding in putting a stop to the capers of a drunken cossack who has irreverently been singing a jaunty (and authentic) folk tune.[1] It is an irony which touches upon the fascination which, as we saw, Tchaikovsky had for Bizet's Carmen, who is murdered while the joyous singing of the crowd at the bullfight in the background resounds. The inebriated cossack's conscious dissociation—he is defiantly indifferent to the chopping off of the landowners' heads—even if partly a manifestation of the alcohol, is a kind of obverse of the ignorance of the crowd in Bizet's opera, who can take no conscious decision as to whether or not they care about Carmen's being killed; they simply do not know about it. The scene of the Shrovetide revelers in Act 4 of Serov's opera *The Power of the Fiend*, premiered in 1871, in which the inebriated hero-villain, Pëtr, sings a song to the accompaniment of the balalaika, before suddenly becoming infuriated with and attempting to kill a boy, Vasia, has been identified by Taruskin as a likely influence on the incident of the drunken cossack in *Mazeppa*.

As the execution procession in *Mazeppa* gradually appears, a balefully great volume of sound is built up through antiphonal exchanges between the orchestra and the band, augmented by the chorus's exclamations: "The hour of execution is nigh! The terrible hour is nigh!" (The use of a band in such a dramatic setting is a feature typical of grand opera.) This almost overwhelming mass of sound contrasts movingly with the vulnerability and dignity of the two victims, who are brought onstage and sing a prayer of repentance to God on their knees. This is a still more powerful use of music broadly in the pattern of Russian Orthodox liturgical chant than that in *The Maid of Orléans* (the people's hymn, initiated by Joan, in Act 1) or even *The Oprichnik* (the oprichniks' highly atmospheric offstage chorus at the start of Act 2 scene 2), furthering the grand-opera manner of evoking religious connotations for stage effect. The melody of the prayer, sung mostly by Kochubei, with whose voice Iskra presently joins, in unison, is constricted in range of pitch (a typical liturgical chant characteristic). By not using a wide range of pitch, but concentrating mostly on just a few adjacent tones, such music conveys a lessening of the human ego and a devotional quality. However, when Kochubei and Iskra continue the prayer by singing of passing "to that place where there is no sorrow," a sudden melodic blossoming occurs. Now the range of pitch becomes very broad indeed. Abraham wrote of the most distinctive of Tchaikovsky's melodies, such as the D flat major theme that opens the First Piano Concerto, as being "marked by leaps rather than steps, moving boldly up and down like handwriting full of character."[2] A special permutation of this occurs here. Tchaikovsky reserves his most characteristic melodic writing for the prayer's most significant words, namely, "no sorrow," which shift onto a strongly profiled arch of melody, after the stepwise movement that came up to this point. That same melodic arch is then used in a sequence, being restated in total at a lower pitch, and then, although very modified in shape, repeated at a still-lower pitch. The formalization to which this melody is thereby submitted prevents the sudden sense of release that it at first conveys from seeming in any way exaggerated. The victims' humility is, instead, underlined.

Furthermore, Tchaikovsky's emulation of the restricted pitch-range of Russian Orthodox liturgical chant, followed by an evocation of freedom through the contrast with his much more individualistic melodic writing, with its roots in European art-music, may be compared to his combination of folk-derived and Western styles. Brown has shown that Tchaikovsky developed a powerful synthesis, in his most typical compositions, of elements of Russian folksong—the sense of inertia that comes from its characteristic repetitiveness and constriction in range of pitch—and the harmonic drive of the European art-music tradition.[3] This often produced effects not dissimilar to those in the present scene in *Mazeppa*.

The chorus immediately repeats Kochubei and Iskra's prayer. There develops, therefore—instead of an ensemble-chorus at the critical turning point in a drama, of the kind that we observed in *The Oprichnik*, *Eugene Onegin*, and *The Maid of Orléans*—a notably different, but nevertheless related, use of musical forces at the comparable dramatic juncture in this opera: a pair of voices echoed by the chorus. In terms of the plot, perhaps the closest comparison is with *Onegin*, for Lensky, before the ensemble-chorus that ends Act 2 scene 1 in that work, makes himself vulnerable by desiring revenge above all else, and challenging his friend, over what was merely a petulant prank (the flirtation with Olga), to the duel. Lensky, of course, paid dearly for that, and while, on the other hand, Mazeppa does not pay by losing his life for the atrocity of executing Kochubei (his wife's father) and Iskra, his need for vengeance upon them is essentially as self-blinding. Perhaps the collapse of Mazeppa's fortunes, as marked by the ensuing Act 3 entr'acte's symboliza-tion of Peter the Great's victory at Poltava, can be seen as confirming this execution as his defining act of overreaching. Instead of the rich interplay of voices in the crucial ensemble-choruses of the three earlier operas, some-thing much leaner and starker is employed here: The intertwining of several voices in an ensemble is replaced by the pair of voices in unison, and there is no mixing of Kochubei and Iskra's singing with that of the chorus (whereas the ensemble had been combined with the chorus in the three antecedents).

After the beheading itself, at the very moment of which Kochubei's wife, Liubov, and Maria, rush onstage, too late to try to prevent the disaster, the final gesture of Act 2 is allotted to the orchestra, which forcefully repeats the melody of the executed men's prayer, like the loud raising of a lament, but perhaps also auguring Mazeppa's impending rout.

That certainly seems an impressive reversal of the musical scenario at the end of the immediately preceding scene (Act 2 scene 2), for there, while Liubov and Maria had desperately rushed to get to the execution to forestall it, the orchestra had proclaimed a brief outburst of Mazeppa's grimly incisive leitmotif (first heard at the start of the opera's Overture), denoting the hetman's temporary ascendancy. The final occurrence in the opera of his once-mighty leitmotif, now appropriately furtive and dwindling in volume to *pianissimo*, comes near the end of Act 3 as he runs away, his political world in ruins, and his personal one also, as he has witnessed the collapse of his wife's sanity.

Maria's situation at the opera's close is far more dire than Mazeppa's, and to depict her tragedy, Tchaikovsky partly employs, but also very fruitfully develops, the convention established in early nineteenth-century Italian opera in order to depict a character's madness. The first hints of Maria's mental disintegration come in the scene with her mother in Act 2. Mazeppa has kept from her all knowledge of Kochubei's incarceration and imminent beheading. Liubov, having slipped into the hetman's palace at grave risk and assuming Maria knows of her father's plight, begs her daughter to intercede on his behalf to prevent the execution. Dazed but horrified, Maria replies, "What father? What execution?" Those words are accompanied by three flutes playing an obsessively repeated pattern of chords in close harmony. Her mother, still not seeing that Maria genuinely does not comprehend, becomes more vehement in her pleas. Maria exclaims, "Either I have lost my mind, or these are daydreams?"—to which comes a brief, plaintive response from a cor anglais. These woodwind parts relate to the tradition most famously represented in *Lucia di Lammermoor*, premiered in 1835, by Gaet-ano Donizetti (1797–1848) in which Lucia's mad scene has a prominent role for solo flute (Tchaikovsky's use of a trio of flutes develops the convention). The similar scene for the heroine in *Il pirata*, premiered in 1827, by Vincenzo

Bellini (1801–35) features a part for solo cor anglais. The deranged characters are thus provided with a special sound-world to live in, through being associated with a particular instrumental timbre, and that may also embody a sense of sympathy for them. In Tchaikovsky's opera, as Liubov, realizing her daughter's bewilderment is no pretense, relates what has happened to Kochubei up to then, the stress imposed by the information makes Maria faint. Then there comes a particularly effective moment, highlighting through contrast the previous use of tone colors, for the delicate woodwind sounds that had been used earlier to depict the frailty of Maria's mind are now, so to speak, supplanted by the distant menace of the execution procession's offstage band, with its brassy depth and fullness. Above this, Liubov's detached, desperate phrases ring out. She must rouse her daughter. When Maria comes to and they eventually arrive at the horrifying beheading already described, it seems havoc is caused in her mind, for when we next see her, in the latter part of Act 3, her sanity is broken.

This masterly conclusion to the opera introduces Maria onstage with the sound of a succession of brief woodwind solos: bassoon, clarinet, oboe and flute, and then the same instruments in reverse order, perhaps allowing things to come full circle to represent her thoughts being trapped in a delusional state. An equally original stroke seems to come with the use immediately afterwards of a solo violin, its distinctively warm timbre appearing to extend more sympathy to the unfortunate heroine than had been the case with the early nineteenth-century mad scenes, where a solo woodwind was the typical obbligato instrument. The melody the violin plays, however, is a quotation of that which had appeared in the orchestral accompaniment to Maria's entry onstage for her encounter with Mazeppa in Act 2 scene 2, which, as noted earlier, had been the scene that encouraged Tchaikovsky to recommence work on the opera after briefly abandoning it. To this same melody, later in that scene, Maria had declared Mazeppa to be dearer to her than all else. The use in the mad scene of material quoted from earlier in the work is a common feature of the original tradition (*Lucia di Lammermoor* again provides the most celebrated illustration of that procedure). Even more movingly, the melody of Maria's excited exclamation to Mazeppa in Act 2 scene 2 (between the two appearances of the melody we have just mentioned and after he has revealed his political plans to her), that he would become Tsar of his native land, returns in Act 3 as her broken mind can no longer distinguish between her hate and love of him. She tells him to leave her, saying he is ugly and she had mistaken him for another. She describes this other man (and this is where the melody, so strongly associated with Mazeppa, recurs) as "handsome! Love burns in his eyes."

When Mazeppa is presently dissuaded by Orlik from taking Maria with them, she takes on a special and unexpected strength. Left abandoned in a dangerous situation, as Russian soldiers have not long since crossed the stage, with the approach of some other (unspecified) people apparently imminent (as Orlik had reported), the hetman's wife, too deranged to perceive her plight, catches sight of the mortally wounded Andrei (whom Mazeppa had shot). She takes him to be a child and sings him a lullaby. The contrast between Andrei's disjointed phrases as he, still in touch with reality although in his last mortal moments, struggles to make Maria understand he is dying and cannot help her, and her lyrically conjoined phrases as she, separated from reality, tries to lull him to sleep, forms a hauntingly surreal conclusion to this inconsistent but, for all that, great and remarkable work, in which, somewhere amidst the damaged entanglement of humanity, something good survives.

CHAPTER EIGHT

TRAGIC FORCE REAFFIRMED:
THE ENCHANTRESS

FOLLOWING A FAIRLY casual suggestion from Modest Tchaikovsky to his brother, early in 1885, concerning how suitable for operatic treatment the scene of the hero and heroine's dramatic meeting in Ippolit Shpazhinsky's new play *The Enchantress* might be, the composer, at that time eagerly looking yet again for opera subjects, wrote to its author. Shpazhinsky undertook to transform his tragedy (which has a historical period-setting for a fictional plot, whereas *Mazeppa*, as we saw, had roots at any rate in the interaction of actual personages in history) into a libretto. The story, which is even grimmer than that of *Mazeppa*, unfolds in the Nizhny-Novgorod area in the final quarter of the fifteenth century. As adapted in the opera, it is as follows:

Act 1: The courtyard of a tavern, by the ferry crossing at the confluence of the rivers Oka and Volga, with Nizhny-Novgorod in the distance. Folk are carousing and making merry. The tavern's carefree, life-loving hostess, Nastasia, affectionately called "Kuma" (meaning "godmother"), faces a grave problem. She is warned that the puritanical old clerk, Mamyrov, disapproving of the revelries at her establishment, has vowed to bring his master, the governor-general himself, Prince Nikita Kurliatev, to witness what happens here.

Called upon for a song, Kuma sings a heartfelt arioso about "Mother Volga." The governor-general's son, Prince Iury, and huntsman Zhuran, with others, coming back from the hunt, approach in boats on the river. Agitated, Kuma suddenly shows the opposite type of feelings, for her friend Polia wonders what Iury might be like, and she replies with an enraptured account of him. The crowd shout out their greetings, but Iury regrets he cannot join them, although Zhuran does come ashore. The boats move away. Zhuran asks Kuma why she had fallen silent and had not invited Iury to disembark. She reveals she had been embarrassed. Just then, news is given that the governor-general has been spotted, drawing close to the tavern. Kuma succeeds in assuaging the general alarm that ensues. Prince Nikita enters with Mamyrov, guards, and others. Mamyrov states a fierce condemnation of this den of iniquity, rather anomalously amplified by one of the transgressors present, the drunken vagrant monk Paisy, who calls Kuma's tavern (to the crowd's outrage) Sodom itself. The prince summons the hostess. Kuma defends herself with dignity, and Nikita is at once taken with her charms. Mamyrov excoriates her for dressing seductively despite being a widow. The crowd lambast him, but Kuma deftly silences them, pointing out that the prince surely does not need their intervention to judge the truth. Nikita is further impressed by her, musing to himself that she is "even majestic!" She skillfully defuses Mamyrov's charges about every manner of excess at her tavern.

Even when Nikita puts an accusation to her of practicing evil magic, she quashes this by observing that her sorcery is merely to welcome people kindly, and that here they may leave their worries behind them.

She clearly senses she is gaining ground, and offers the prince a sip of wine. He calls her a "wily one" as he falls beneath the spell of her shrewd hospitality. Mamyrov's frustration grows, and he tries again to bring the prince round to his side, but gets an angry response from him. Having enjoyed his drink, Prince Nikita gives Kuma a precious gift—he takes off his ring and throws it into the freshly drained goblet.

Amid general amazement, there immediately follows a "decimet (a cappella) with chorus" (an ensemble of ten singers, comprising Kuma, Prince Nikita, Mamyrov, and seven minor characters, including Zhuran and Polia, with choral support, but without any instrumental accompaniment). In this, Kuma sings of her being overjoyed at the prince's gift, Nikita is deeply enraptured by her, Mamyrov expresses shame at the situation, and the others are impressed by the gift and comment upon Mamyrov's misjudgment.

Emboldened at the turn of events, Kuma begins to overstep the situation, rather impudently offering Mamyrov wine, which provokes him to curse her furiously to himself. Kuma summons a group of wandering minstrel-clowns (*skomorokhi*) for the prince's entertainment. Nikita asks Mamyrov if he would like to watch them, to which he replies sourly. Kuma suggests to the prince that his clerk be made to dance with the minstrel-clowns. Nikita presently orders him to do so, and the hapless Mamyrov, in a parody of dancing, is spun round and round by Kuma's uncle, Foka, to the crowd's laughter.

Act 2: The garden of Prince Nikita's home; morning. The prince's wife, Evpraksia, is sitting in the porch. Problems are afoot, and when Mamyrov enters, the princess demands to be told the truth. He informs her of the events that occurred at the tavern, which Prince Nikita now frequents, and alleges that Kuma is Nikita's lover, hinting that she has used sorcery to capture his heart. Describing Kuma as a "witch," Mamyrov recommends that she be gotten rid of, but Evpraksia commands that Mamyrov keep the situation under surveillance. She reviles her husband and turns hysterical. Before departing, Mamyrov tells his sister Nenila, the princess's maid, who is currently attending her, to take matters in hand lest Prince Nikita come. Nenila tries to console her mistress with advice about the use of magic to curb a husband's faithlessness. The princess contemptuously orders her out. Once alone, she vows vengeance upon Kuma.

Iury appears. His mother feigns cheerfulness, but to little avail. Iury will not be distracted from an awareness of something being wrong within the family by her conversation about the bride she and Nikita have chosen for him (a matter he seems, at present, obediently to accept). Evpraksia, for Iury's sake, is evasive about the problems with Kuma. She departs, leaving his questions—he suspects his father may be at the root of her problems—unanswered.

Paisy appears, followed shortly afterwards by Mamyrov; Iury departs. Mamyrov commands Paisy's help to go and spy for him on Kuma's tavern. Paisy exits, and Mamyrov, alone, voices his bitterness at having been made by his master to act the minstrel-clown at Kuma's hostelry. Nikita appears and orders Mamyrov to send for the princess. The clerk leaves. The governor-general sings of his obsessive desire for Kuma. Evpraksia enters, and a fierce argument develops over her husband's alleged infidelity. She and Nikita depart the stage in opposite directions.

Distant commotion suddenly occurs. One of Nikita's huntsmen climbs over the fence into the garden, carrying a bloodstained knife. Stones are thrown after him. From his pursuers are heard cries of accusation of murder. Two more of the governor-general's servants clamber over the fence, narrowly escaping the mob, who then break their way through into the garden. Mamyrov confronts them, supported by others of Nikita's faction. He orders the invaders seized, and, amidst fighting, Iury enters and intercedes.

Kichiga, who is the invaders' ringleader and a frequenter of Kuma's tavern, explains to Iury that the governor-general's retainers steal from them, and there is no redress. Iury shows compassion and sends the intruders home.

The princess, Nenila, and Paisy appear. Iury is criticized by them and Mamyrov for having encroached upon his father's duties. In response to Iury's question as to his father's whereabouts, Paisy reveals that he is at Kuma's, which provokes an outraged declaration from the princess that she will rush there herself and break up their embraces. She is too shocked to reply to her son's question: Is his father dishonoring her? Nenila, however, observes that Kuma will be the death of the princess. Iury vows to kill

Kuma. His mother is enraptured, and Mamyrov, Paisy, and Nenila look forward to Kuma's destruction.

Act 3:   Kuma's cottage. Alternately amorous and despairing, Prince Nikita makes futile advances to Kuma. He shows jealous anger at her revelation that she loves another, but she does not name him. He gives her a forceful embrace, from which she tears herself free. Taking a knife and holding it to her throat, she exclaims, "I'd sooner die than surrender!" Declaring that they "will not part alive," but also that he will have his way, he makes a dramatic exit. She is apprehensive of his discovering that she loves his son.

Polia rushes in, with the news that Princess Evpraksia has heard about Nikita and Kuma, and that Iury has sworn to kill the alleged mistress. Foka enters, warning his niece that she also faces accusations of ensnaring the princess's husband with sorcery. Kuma is astonished that Iury believed this. Polia and Foka warn her to arrange to be guarded; Polia departs. Astonishingly, Kuma tells her uncle not to call anyone in. He is anxious that Iury might come to murder her. "Well then, he'll be welcome," she replies. Suspecting she has gone mad, Foka leaves.

Presently, Kuma is seized with alarm when, through the window, she sees movement beyond. Two figures, one of them Iury, are approaching. She seeks the refuge of her bed and from there listens. Iury appears with Zhuran. Iury draws back the curtain of the bed, to find Kuma lying there attractively leaning on one hand and looking at him boldly. He drops his dagger and backs away, covering his eyes. She declares she knew of his intentions, but did not arrange for any guards to protect her. He accuses her of coming between his parents. She tells Zhuran peremptorily to be off, and, at a sign from Iury, he leaves.

Kuma proceeds to tell Iury of his father's lustful advances toward her and of the terrible threat he issued. Iury is loath to believe this. She swears to God it is the truth, and she covers his hand with kisses in supplication. He tries to disengage his hand. She notices the dagger he dropped and returns it to him. He declares he had drawn it to protect himself from ambush. Summoning extra courage, she finally declares her love openly and fully to him. He is overcome with apprehension and would leave, but she presses her avowal. He suddenly proclaims himself to be her protector, and again makes to depart, but she restrains him, asking why he wants to leave. He accuses her of foolishness. She exclaims that it would have been better if he had stabbed her. When she begins to sob bitterly at his expression of pity for her, he suddenly reveals that it is not just pity that has kept him here. She begs to know what. He declares his love. Their impassioned duet ends Act 3.

Act 4:   A somber, dense forest, amid hills, with the bank of the river Oka visible through the trees on the left. Offstage horn calls are heard. A new character enters, the sorcerer Kudma. Angry at being disturbed, he goes back into his cave. Zhuran and fellow huntsmen appear; he stays to await Iury, and the others depart to hunt. Iury enters, and Zhuran, who has made the arrangements for Kuma to escape with Iury, nevertheless advises him against this elopement. Iury reveals that it took one glance to fall in love and that for love to fade it would take eternity. If he stays, he adds, he will be forced into the marriage his parents have arranged. Abandoning the escape is impossible. Iury and Zhuran exit to join the hunt.

The princess, who is in the guise of a pilgrim, appears with Paisy. She has come to procure from the sorcerer a way to rid her son of Kuma. She meets Kudma outside his cave; Paisy runs away as he appears. Evpraksia obtains from Kudma what she specifically wants: a poison to cause searing pain before the victim dies.

Kuma arrives by boat with several associates, including Kichiga. Her friends return to the boat to keep watch in case they have been followed. Kuma sings of her longing for Iury. The princess comes out of the cave, sees Kuma, and feels Fate has sent her into her hands. She presents herself to Kuma as a pilgrim traveling on a pilgrimage, whose companions have lagged behind and for whom she will wait here. She comments with deep irony on Kuma's beauty, which is such that "even a prince would be glad to run off" with her. Kuma stumbles for words to reply to this, and the princess offers to refresh her with water from a nearby spring. Evpraksia fetches the water, to which she has furtively added the poison. Kuma drinks it, commenting on its bitter taste. The sorcerer's sinister laughter rings out.

The sound of offstage horn calls is heard. The princess exits. Iury appears, and he and Kuma embrace, singing that, together again, they are done with their troubles. To the relish of Evpraksia and the sorcerer in the background, the poison begins to take its effect. Kuma reveals that she had drunk some water. The princess steps forward to reveal herself as the one who gave it, declaring that she has washed away her family's disgrace. Iury calls his mother a murderess. As the huntsmen reappear, Kuma dies. The grief-stricken Iury is led aside by Zhuran. Evpraksia quietly orders the huntsmen to dispose of the body in the river. Iury turns round too late to prevent this. The princess moves away. He despairs.

Prince Nikita arrives by boat, with his attendants, as it grows dark. He was informed of Kuma's earlier departure on the river and now demands that his son tell him where she is hidden. He interprets as trickery Iury's statement that she is dead, and he points to her belongings (brought there when she arrived) as evidence. Iury states that nobody else but his father is Kuma's murderer. Nikita stabs his son. Declaring that that act has united him with Kuma forever, Iury dies. Reappearing, Evpraksia, horrified, throws herself upon his body. The attendants, troubled by the scene, gather round. Thunder resounds in the distance.

A male chorus of mourning is sung for Iury. Amidst the breaking storm, Prince Nikita, overcome with horror at what he has done and denounced by the sorcerer, goes mad.

The Enchantress, composed from 1885 to 1887, was first performed at the Mariinsky Theater on 1 November 1887, conducted by Tchaikovsky himself. Initial public interest in the work soon waned. Subsequent new productions in Tiflis, almost two months after the premiere, and in Moscow, in February 1890, did not portend the establishing of *The Enchantress* as a repertory opera, and it fell into neglect.

Shpazhinsky evidently did not "feel" the essential differences between opera and spoken drama, with the result that the libretto he produced is verbose and contains a substantial number of minor characters, which may cause distractions in opera. When text is sung, the words are far less discernible to the ear than when spoken, and the function of certain of these figures may, therefore, not come through as clearly as the author wished. (The above synopsis does not give the roles of all the minor players.) Nevertheless, Shpazhinsky's story itself has remarkable cogency, building with an inexorable sense of the characters' deteriorating personal situation and of their attempts to reassert themselves with actions that exceed the bounds of what might actually remedy their predicament. Tchaikovsky responded to this with a profoundly inspired and dramatically well-structured score that lacks the weaknesses of *Mazeppa*, but consistently matches its creative strengths.

To articulate various parts of the plot, Tchaikovsky further employed the tense, emotionally heavy musical language that he had evolved to depict Byron's tragic figure, the eponymous hero of the *Manfred* Symphony, which was composed immediately before *The Enchantress*. To counterbalance such potently gloomy music, there is, once again, considerable and rich use of Russian folk style, revealing that the composer was still, even in his late period, fully in touch with its open-hearted and life-enhancing lyricism. And the bleak horrors of the final Act of *The Enchantress* are both offset and underlined, as we shall see, by a procedure involving folk music whose antecedents are in *Eugene Onegin*.

A lively folk tableau is built up in Act 1 for the revelry in Kuma's tavern. Among its felicitous touches is a scene using quintuple meter (in which guests arriving at Kuma's greet their hostess) with resonances of Glinka, like, also, the five-time girls' chorus in the first Act of *Mazeppa*. Two known folk songs, "A blue-gray dove flew at dawn" and "It is not a noise that makes the noise," are adapted in Kuma's lyrical arioso about Mother Volga (and had also been used in the Overture). When the puritanical Mamyrov, elderly clerk to the governor-general, Prince Nikita, arrives, bringing his master to see the iniquities of Kuma's establishment, Kuma knows she must summon every effort to prevent her tavern's closure. Her flirtatious and courageous winning-over of the governor-general is pure pragmatism—and it carries a price, which nobody at the time can see. Prince Nikita falls head over heels with desire for her; she has no such feelings for him, even though she is prepared to encourage him for the sake of preserving her livelihood.

The seed of the ensuing tragedy lies in the governor-general's observation that Kuma is "even majestic!" No doubt, he is not drawn to her only for her beauty, but because her pride reflects a feature that had also drawn him to his wife. Princess Evpraksia's pride is of the type which may contain a forcefully jealous nature, and indeed, that jealousy prevents the princess not only from tolerating her husband's involvement with the tavern hostess, but also leads her to cause Kuma's death when it becomes clear that, later on, she has become involved with their son. Kuma's pride spills over into hubris at the strength of her own power to enchant a man, for after she successfully uses it to defeat Mamyrov's attempt to cause her trouble, she reacts too surely to the grateful token of that enchantment which Nikita then gives her: the gift of the ring from his finger. Emboldened by this, she incites the governor-general to force his clerk to dance with the skomorokhi. Mamyrov gains his own, ultimately devastating, revenge when he stirs up Evpraksia's jealousy, alleging that Nikita has Kuma for his lover (which in fact is merely the governor-general's ardent wish).

The opera's first Act is made to function like a depressed spring, whose latent energy will be set free in the closing Act. The musical gesture that, with a dramatically sure sense of exaggeration, depresses that spring, is the decimet with chorus, which opens the Act's finale. A slight, but ominous, release of the spring's tension comes with Mamyrov's humiliation amidst the dancing skomorokhi, whose folk-influenced music displays a well-judged degree of overstated vivacity (an externalized symbol of Kuma's hubris).

The decimet is a new departure in Tchaikovsky's work. There is no precedent for such a rich ensemble texture in any of his previous operas. However, this item, with its accompanying parts for chorus, follows as an imaginative development of the ensemble-choruses that had so potently embodied the turning point in the plot in his earlier operas. Moreover, there are three vital new factors in addition to the greater proliferation of individual vocal parts (the ten here being made possible by the presence of so many minor characters, which is perhaps the only exception to the point that Shpazhinsky's libretto is unduly laden with minor roles). First, the decimet with chorus is entirely free of instrumental accompaniment. Second, and even more important, its location within the design of *The Enchantress*, in the closing stages of Act 1 (the opening item of the finale to that Act, there being two further items: a "Scene and Chorus" and a "Dance of the Skomorokhi and Scene") is earlier than that of the ensemble-choruses of *The Oprichnik* (finale to Act 3), *Eugene Onegin* (finale to Act 2 scene 1), *The Maid of Orléans* (finale to Act 3), and the corresponding (although, as we saw in the assessment of the opera concerned, also notably different) pair of voices in unison, succeeded by chorus in the execution scene of *Mazeppa* (finale to Act 2 scene 3). Finally, and most significantly, the dramatic context in *The Enchantress* is of an unsustainably great, general sense of triumph, whereas at the points specified in the above operas, events unfold that are very obviously grave.

The cited item in *Mazeppa*, although opposite in context to the present decimet with chorus, has in common with it the fervent use of unaccompanied vocal music. There, the chorus, in a prayer commending the souls of Kochubei and Iskra to God on the verge of their execution, had sung initially with only very bare accompaniment: periodic chords from the orchestra with entirely unaccompanied choral sound set between them. The item in *The Enchantress* occurs so unusually early in the opera because the dramatic situation it represents will erupt much more forcefully if given extra time to gestate. This decimet with chorus is, in a sense, a secular prayer, as it relates to an atmosphere of worldly well-being that cannot ultimately last. The gift of Prince Nikita's ring is such an apparently complete reversal of the likely outcome of events (the closing down of the tavern) that it creates a euphoric displacement of expected disaster with present joy. But its foundation is false, as regards Kuma's purely flirtatious enchantment of the governor-general. To reflect this, Tchaikovsky creates a kind of island of musical enchantment, as the decimet with chorus, expressing the enraptured feelings of all at the new situation (bar Mamyrov, who laments the shame of it) rises up, in the sustained luxury of its unbroken vocal sound, from the sea of voices mixed with instruments that had taken us up to it.

The orchestral cadences that bring the curtain down on Act 1, concluding the dance of the skomorokhi with the derided clerk in their midst, contain hints of the parallel minor form of the major key that had conveyed the dance (A major with C natural and F natural intruding). Although subtle, these darker sounds are an ominous pointer to the impending tragedy.

The entr'acte to Act 2 presents the first of the succession of references to the *Manfred* Symphony's turbulent musical language, oiling the wheels of tragedy. The actual material of the entr'acte anticipates that of the scene, early in Act 2, of Princess Evpraksia's fit of hysterics after Mamyrov's assertion to her that her husband and Kuma are lovers. A lyrical and folk-like fragment of melody is presented in ever quicker note values, and it becomes increasingly distorted, culminating in a series of wild flurries of notes of extremely short duration, separated by fleeting silences. This method of development relates directly back to the coda of the *Manfred* Symphony's first movement, where similar means were used to convey Manfred's desire for oblivion. This incident in the entr'acte leads to a reprise of the folk-like theme, now partly transformed into a proud, art-music shape, with extravagant melodic leaps that were not in it previously. It is this latter passage that recurs for the scene of Evpraksia's terrible fit, the mixture of folk and sophisticated melodic styles perhaps representing the princess's desire to triumph over that person who is of the people: Kuma. Tchaikovsky restricted the graphic portrayal of hysteria (the bursts of quick notes) to the entr'acte, possibly through a sense of compassion for Evpraksia. In the scene itself, the princess's anger is disproportionate to anything that might help her case, and she shows hubris in her despising of her maid Nenila's well-meant, if rather maladroit, attempts to sympathize with her and suggest how magic might be employed to bring Nikita back to her arms. When she presently confronts the governor-general, Evpraksia denounces him and brushes aside his denials of his amorous pursuits—"It is not nonsense, but shame and sin, disgrace!"—to a melody whose setting shows just how encompassed by jealous anger she has become. Her melodic line is reproduced, in fairly standard fashion, at the pitch at which she actually sings it, in a woodwind doubling, but that melody is also sounded at the octave beneath (on a clarinet and bassoon in unison), and thereby passes below the accompanying harmony (which is on tremolo strings) and circumvents the usual structure in art-music of an independent bass line supporting the overall texture. The natural (or, at any rate, traditional) order of things is being bent, so to speak, to her will, in its potentially uncontrollable and alarming state. When their ominous clash of wills reaches its peak, and Nikita and Evpraksia, each fiercely holding to their original stand in this matter, quit the stage in opposite directions, the orchestra comments with augmented triads. That is a stroke that pertains, as we saw in regard to *The Oprichnik*, to Glinka's whole-tone-scale method of depicting evil (but appears in the present instance as the use of actual chords, rather than the outlining of the harmony melodically, as at the close of that earlier opera). Tchaikovsky seems to be saying that nothing good can come of this situation.

Indeed, this orchestral postlude to Nikita and Evpraksia's encounter goes on to foreshadow the start of the next scene, with an insistence that begins to be unusual, upon a harmony that had a particularly significant role in the *Manfred* Symphony. What matters about this type of harmonic structure, a minor chord with an added major sixth, is the sense of emotional pain it can convey. It was, in itself, a well-established element of Romantic-period harmony and, in the context of Tchaikovsky's output it had appeared, for example, to accompany the actual moment of Andrei's death in *Mazeppa*. In the first movement of *Manfred*, however, its exceptionally extensive use had emphasized the despair of that work's hero. Here, as the chord persists from the musical aftermath of the argument between Nikita and Evpraksia into the start of the next scene (which begins without any break), its extended usage becomes fraught with tension. It becomes clear that Tchaikovsky is underlining a parallel between the disorder in the inner world of the prince and princess's marriage, and chaos in society at large. For now comes the scene of the vengeful mob chasing a huntsman of Nikita's who has murdered one of them into the governor-general's garden, smashing through its fence in pursuit. When Iury presently emerges, he overreaches himself by quelling the disarray (which is properly the business of his father, even though he is, significantly, absent) to the accompaniment of the same emotive chord (of A minor with an added F sharp) that had so effectively led into the scene and opened it. "Away with you!" he says to his father's retainers, who had unsuccessfully attempted to overpower the intruders, and to the latter he extends tolerance, instructing them to return home. The chord conveys an augury, for it already has associations of death, as it was a murder that had caused the riotous invasion of the governor-general's property. The identical chord returns at an important point in the finale to Act 2. The context is the revelation that Nikita's absence is because he is at Kuma's, and Iury's inference (from Evpraksia and Nenila's outraged reactions) that his father is involved in infidelity, which provokes Iury to a declaration about killing Kuma. Between his initial exclamation, "Kill her, kill her!" and his warming to the thought of it—"Kill her and everything is settled, kill her with a single blow!"—comes an emphatic, *sforzando* chord of A minor plus an F sharp. This further foreshadows tragedy. Iury's assumption that he has the right to rectify his mother's woes with such an extreme act has appalling ramifications. Although he does not carry out his pledge, that pledge itself constitutes hubris which, in classic fashion, precedes the hero's fall. Furthermore, the music setting his announcing of his murderous intentions conveys an ecstatic feel. As with Mamyrov's discomfiture among the dancing skomorokhi at the end of Act 1, Tchaikovsky has employed over-emphasized exhilaration to powerful dramatic effect. It is a further press downward on the spring of tragedy, also occurring in the finale of an Act. The tension mounts.

At the start of Act 3, in the scene between Nikita and Kuma, the heroine steadfastly, although with sympathy and even pity, spurns his advances. He is not a man who surrenders easily, however. His chilling threat to her, "Accursed one! We will not part alive," set again within the context of the chord of A minor with an F sharp, is followed by an angular, fierce phrase from the orchestra, repeated sequentially as Nikita leaves, as though his words are ringing in her ears. This music conspicuously recalls the second part of the "motto-theme" of the hero of the *Manfred* Symphony (that is, the melody played by strings after the woodwinds have finished the first part of the theme, at the start of that work).[1]

In the next scene, Kuma, warned by her friend Polia, and uncle Foka, of Iury's murderous vow, decides to face the danger alone. When Iury appears, in the scene that had prompted Modest Tchaikovsky to bring this story to his brother's attention and which was the first part of the opera to be sketched,

Kuma reveals to him the true situation between her and Nikita, and he is gradually overwhelmed with love of her, not just through her beauty but through her courage. However, she is the first to declare her feelings. As she begins her avowal of love, he is seized with apprehension: "Enough! It is time for me to return home." That is understandable, and his outburst is initially accompanied by that very same chord that had attended his father's terrible threat to Kuma. Iury must sense the appalling risks of any involvement with her, for she has already told him of Nikita's threat. His response, as she presses ahead with her declaration, is to try to resolve the situation with a compromise; he exclaims he will henceforth prove to be her "protector." That word brings with it the clarity of a C major chord. But all is not well. The chord of foreboding (A minor plus an F sharp) now immediately recurs, yet again, supplanting the optimistic feel. By implication, however much Iury feels he can be Kuma's guardian, circumstances will prevent it. When Iury, in the face of Kuma's continued protestation of her feelings, declares his reciprocal love, their fate is sealed. The finale to Act 3, their love-duet, therefore also depresses the spring of tragedy, adding cumulatively to the conclusion of Acts 1 and 2. The tragic tensions are about to be released.

Act 4 of *The Enchantress* is a modification of the originally proposed ending. The librettist's initial intention to have the opera run to a fifth Act was rejected by Tchaikovsky as extending the narrative to a degree that was unsustainable in sung drama. The present Act 4 is, consequently, a condensation of the previously envisaged Acts 4 and 5. The resulting pace of events is much quicker than in the rest of the opera and powerfully conveys the sense of nemesis, of terrible actions succeeding one another with seemingly unstoppable momentum. At a location by the river Oka, the princess poisons Kuma as she and Iury are on the point of eloping. Iury is killed by his own father, who presently arrives and disbelieves Iury's statement that Kuma is dead. As Evpraksia had ordered the disposal of the corpse in the river, there is, indeed, no immediate evidence to support Iury. The princess faces the horror of returning to the scene just as her son is dying. The governor-general, his mind engulfed by the enormity of what he has done, loses his sanity while around him nature produces the parallel enormity of a raging storm. A dynamically sustained orchestral climax, strongly recalling the music from *Francesca da Rimini* in which Tchaikovsky had depicted the tempests in hell punishing those who had given way to lust (the satisfaction of Nikita's having been denied him by Kuma—another kind of hell), brings *The Enchantress* to its close. What would, in other circumstances, simply have been histrionic, is instead a consummately judged setting-free of the accumulated dramatic tensions of the opera. The forces originally held back by the decimet with chorus in Act 1, that utopia that could not last, are now devastatingly revealed. [2]

To help compensate for the comfortless feel of the work's ending, Tchaikovsky precedes this tragic Act 4 with an entr'acte of special expressive intent. The opening measures present this orchestral interlude's main theme, an authentic folk song, "Serëzha the shepherd," which Tchaikovsky had himself collected at Maidanovo, where he had recently settled after all the wanderings abroad and in Russia that had followed the collapse of his marriage. It is a melody of extrovert innocence, presented in a notably plain form: in simple octaves, the tune duplicating itself, and unaccompanied by any harmony. It is immediately followed by a jarring succession of loud, disjointed chords, separated by glaring silences. The effect, considered in solely musical terms, is patently crude. However, one is reminded of Liadov's observation, quoted at the start of this book, regarding Tchaikovsky's lack of fear of disapproval.[3] That characteristic enabled him here to symbolize, simultaneously, the gratuitous nature of tragedy itself and the imperturbable security of the folk ethos, for the story goes on to imply at least that the ordinary folk—as exemplified by Kuma's companions who bring her by boat to her ill-fated rendezvous with Iury—will continue with their lives after the tragic events have been expended. So, ultimately, the crashing chords can be seen as having safely evaporated into their own rhetorical silences. Indeed, when the heroine's associates row her in, although she is now on the very verge of the tragedy, the same folk melody returns, in a brief orchestral interlude, not now interspersed by violent chords, but, rather, by a depiction of birdcalls in the woodwind instruments. The continuity of nature itself is emphasized. Amid the despair there are glimmers of light. In these treatments, Tchaikovsky furthers the dramatic potential that he had so fruitfully explored in *Eugene Onegin*, of the juxtaposition of folk-based and art-music styles.[4] For example, in essence, the shepherds' pipings at dawn in that opera, after the tensions of Tatiana's sleepless night spent writing her letter to the hero, anticipate the even more effective usage of the stylistic contrasts here—more effective because more necessary, in view of the present tale's sheer grimness.

CHAPTER NINE

PUSHKIN REVISITED AND A DRAMATIC CATHARSIS: THE QUEEN OF SPADES

TCHAIKOVSKY'S LIBRETTIST FOR *The Queen of Spades* was his own brother, Modest, whose text, based on Pushkin's short story of the same title, was substantially modified by the composer. Prior to the brothers' joint venture, Modest had been preparing the libretto, to a commission from the Imperial Theaters, to be set by the composer Nikolai Klenovsky (1857–1915), and it was passed, after the latter withdrew from the project, firstly to Nikolai Solovëv (1846–1916). When he too declined to write the music, the still-incomplete libretto was recommended by the Imperial Theaters' director, Ivan Vsevolozhsky, to Pëtr Tchaikovsky himself.

The hero of Pushkin's tale, the young military officer Hermann, a serious figure of German origin, gives up a careful abstinence from gambling in favor of a sudden obsessive pursuit of it once he has learned that a secret exists for a winning formula of three cards that might bring fabulous wealth. The secret had been revealed many years previously to a now aged countess. Hermann sets out to discover it from her. The time of the opera's action as decided, in consultation with Modest, by the administration of the Imperial Theaters, along with a number of other changes, was set at the end of the reign of Catherine the Great in the late eighteenth century (rather than in the early nineteenth century as in Pushkin's original). The libretto unfolds as follows:

Act 1 scene 1: St. Petersburg, a quadrangle in the Summer Garden; a spring day. After a chorus of boys playing soldier, and a chorus of their governesses, the gambler Chekalinsky and Surin, a Horse Guards officer, talk of the odd character of Hermann, a penniless Engineers officer. All the previous night, he had seemed "chained" to the gaming table—but only to watch others gamble. Hermann now appears, somber and pale, with Count Tomsky, another Horse Guards officer.

Hermann reveals his obsessional love for a woman who, being noble-born, is beyond any realistic hopes of attainability. Only death would remain, he declares, if Fate's decree is that he cannot have her. Prince Eletsky enters. He confirms to Surin that he has become engaged. After a duet in which Eletsky exults in his good fortunes, and Hermann, to himself, deplores *his* bad fortunes, Tomsky and Hermann ask the identity of the prince's betrothed. She has just appeared; it is Liza. She is with her grandmother, the countess. Hermann turns still more morose. Liza and the countess feel foreboding at seeing Hermann with his strange air once again; he has similar feelings about the Countess. Tomsky escorts the countess away and returns alone. Eletsky enthuses to Liza about the portents for their happiness. That makes Hermann reflect, wryly, that God counterbalanced fair weather with thunder. A clap of thunder rolls in the distance.

Surin and Chekalinsky deride the old countess as a witch. Tomsky relates she was once dubbed "The Queen of Spades," and, to their amazement, adds how she had had to give up phenomenal success at gambling. As a young woman in Paris, although called "The Muscovite Venus," the countess preferred faro to love. Tomsky sings a ballad relating how the countess, losing all at the gaming table one day, was offered by Count Saint-Germain a winning formula of three cards in exchange for a "single rendezvous." A day later, she won back with the three cards all she had lost. But after she told her husband the card formula and a handsome young man learned it, a specter appeared that night and told her, "You will receive a mortal stroke from the third one who, ardently and passionately in love, comes to learn from you, by force, the three cards." Surin scoffs at her finding any lover now. Chekalinsky ironically proposes that here is Hermann's gambling opportunity. He and Surin taunt Hermann by echoing the apparition's words, then leave. A storm breaks. The crowd scatters but Hermann remains. He repeats the specter's warning, but declares the card formula is useless to him anyway, as all is finished for him now. He makes a solemn apostrophe to the storm, vowing that Liza shall be his, "or I'll die!"

Act 1 scene 2:   Liza's room. Liza, playing the harpsichord, and her friend Polina, sing a duet to a poem by Zhukovsky about the close of day, to some other girlfriends. Although it is Liza's engagement day, she is gloomy. Polina sings a deeply melancholy song (to a text by K. Batiushkov), Liza's favorite, about a girl expecting love's raptures, but to whom a grave was fated. After the company sings a lively folk-like song in honor of the betrothed couple (with Liza still pensive), a governess enters to silence the merrymaking, which has provoked the countess. The characters gradually disperse. When Liza is alone, she weeps. She feels unworthy of the prince. Then, addressing the night, she reveals her "dark secret," her love for another, which has put her utterly in his power. Hermann appears in the doors of the balcony. Liza steps back in silent horror. She would leave, but he begs her to stay. He confesses his love; she sheds tears, and as he kisses her hand, a knock is heard at the door. It is the countess. Liza motions Hermann to hide.

The countess asks angrily about the noise and Liza's still being dressed. Liza explains she was sleeplessly pacing the room. Ordering the balcony shut and Liza to bed, the countess departs. Muttering part of the specter's warning about the cards, Hermann shudders at the sudden sense of a cold wind blowing from the grave. It gives him an extra impetus to live, and to win Liza. He pleads his love to her again until she stops begging him to leave and declares her love also.

Act 2 scene 1:   A masquerade ball at the home of a wealthy dignitary; the great hall. Chekalinsky, Surin, and Tomsky muse about Hermann: Is he in love, or obsessed with discovering the secret of the cards? Tomsky doubts Hermann could be so foolish as to be seeking the latter, but Surin has heard him state that he is doing so. Tomsky concedes that once Hermann takes up an idea, he must pursue everything to its conclusion.

Prince Eletsky and Liza enter. He cannot learn from her why she is sad. He sings of his love and anguish at the present sense of distance between them. They exit. Hermann enters. He has a note from Liza, requesting that he meet her after the performance. He fears his longing to gain wealth through the cards and run away with Liza will drive him mad. Surin and Chekalinsky steal up to Hermann and taunt him—is he not the "third one" mentioned in the specter's augury? When he turns round, they have disappeared into the crowd. "I am insane!" he declares.

A pastoral entertainment is then announced, "The Shepherdess's Sincerity." In this, a faithful shepherdess, Prilepa, chooses her true love, Milovzor, over Zlatogor (whose name means "mountain of gold") and the temptation he offers her of fabulous wealth. Hermann broods again about the cards. Surin and Chekalinsky's practical joke seems to have taken root; Hermann ponders whether he indeed fulfills the spectral prophecy. The countess is suddenly before him. They shudder and stare at each other. "Look, your mistress!" cries Surin in a mask. Hermann does not know if it is a demon's or a human being's voice. Liza enters. She gives Hermann a key to let himself, the next day, into a secret staircase leading from the garden of her home into the bedroom of the countess (who will be absent), from which he will pass to her own room. She wishes to resolve matters. She wants to be his alone. He insists, despite her anxiety, that he come today. She acquiesces. Once she is gone, Hermann declares that it is now not his will but that of Fate itself that he learn the three cards. The scene ends with excited preparations to greet the arrival of the Tsaritsa, Catherine the Great.

Act 2 scene 2:   The countess's bedroom [nighttime]. Hermann appears, through a secret door. He alternates between resolution to discover the old woman's secret and concern that he is chasing a mere fantasy, a delirium of his own mind. He moves toward Liza's door, but he is transfixed in front of a portrait of the countess in her youth. He feels it is predestined that either she will cause his death, or he hers. Hearing someone coming, he hides. The countess enters, with a chorus of hangers-on and maids. Liza then appears, with the servant Masha, who has noticed that her mistress is ill at ease; Liza is obliged to acknowledge that "he is coming" and might even be here already. She adds he had ordered it thus, that she has chosen him as her spouse, and that she has become the "obedient, true slave" of he whom Fate has sent her. Liza and Masha exit. The hangers-on and maids begin to put the countess to bed but, silencing their babble, she insists she does not wish to sleep there. They put her in an armchair instead.

The countess begins to bemoan modern times and recalls the grand noblemen and noblewomen who used to sing and dance in her day. She used to sing too. Once she sang before the (French) king himself. She then croons an aria from an opera by André Grétry (1741–1813). She seems to doze, but suddenly orders out the hangers-on and maids. She sings softly again and starts falling asleep. Hermann emerges from his hiding-place. He stands in front of her. She wakes up, moving her lips silently, struck dumb with fear. He begs her not to be afraid; he will not harm her. He has come to beg a favor. He says she knows a secret of three cards. At this, she gets up, and Hermann drops to his knees. He beseeches her, if ever she has known what it feels like to love, to tell her secret to him. If it is connected with an appalling sin, he is prepared to take that sin upon himself. "Reveal it to me," he demands, "speak!" She looks threateningly at him. Calling her an "old witch," he then exclaims he will force her to answer and pulls out a pistol. The countess, without any shot being fired, drops dead of fright. At first feeling that that is mere pretense, he then realizes she has indeed died. Horrified, he believes the specter's prophecy has come true. Liza now enters. Appalled at the countess's death, she demands to know if Hermann caused it. "I did not want her to die," he replies, "I just wanted to know the three cards!" Furious that Hermann had, after all, come after the cards, not her, she fiercely orders him out. She falls, sobbing, onto the countess's body.

Act 3 scene 1:   Hermann's room at the barracks; late evening. It is winter. Hermann reads a letter from Liza, in which she asks for a rendezvous by the embankment. She believes he did not want the countess to die, and she wishes him to resolve her sense of guilt before him. She asks that he come by midnight, otherwise her worst fears will be confirmed. Expressing pity at the plight into which he has put her, along with himself, he tries to find respite in sleep. As he dozes in an armchair, a dream frightens him into awakening. In it he saw, once again, the countess's funeral, and he is now unable to tell whether he can actually hear the church choir (an off-stage chorus is singing at this point) or if it is just the wind. He recalls her corpse winking at him.

Suddenly, there is a knocking at the window, and a shadow appears there. As the door begins to open, he rushes toward it, there to be confronted by the countess's ghost. She says she has come under command, and against her will, to grant his request. He must save Liza, wed her, and these three cards will win in series: three, seven, ace. As the ghost disappears, Hermann, with a mad look, says the card sequence aloud.

Act 3 scene 2:   The Winter Canal; nighttime. Liza, in her arioso, sings of how she has tormented herself with constant thoughts of Hermann. She desperately hopes he will appear by the appointed time, but as midnight strikes and he still has not appeared, she breaks out in terrible reproach, concluding that he is a villain and a murderer after all. She feels she is damned together with him. Hermann appears. Now her feelings swing to the opposite extreme, and they sing a love duet. However, as he urges that they run off together to the gambling house, and explains that the countess was recently with him and named for him the three cards, Liza's anxiety that he has gone insane mounts. She asks: Did he kill her? He says no, but adds, with a strange laugh, that he merely raised his pistol and the old sorceress immediately fell down.

Although reverting temporarily to her earlier anger that she is linked with a murderer, Liza soon rallies her thoughts and begs Hermann to come away with her so she can save him. He pushes her away—in his delirium no longer recognizing her—and flees. She declares herself to be ruined, as he is, and throws herself into the river.

Act 3 scene 3:   A gambling house; suppertime. A chorus of guests and players extols the joys of love, gambling, and wine. Seeking vengeance for Liza's death, Prince Eletsky makes his first-ever visit to this place; he has had a premonition Hermann will come here. Tomsky is asked to sing, and he obliges with a folk-like song about female charms. A gambling song, performed by the general company, ensues. A card game begins. Hermann arrives. Eletsky asks Tomsky if he would be willing to be his second in a duel; he agrees. To general astonishment concerning both of the following matters, Hermann asks to participate in a card game, and he bets the sum of forty thousand. "Surely you have learned the three cards from the countess?" interjects Surin. Hermann does not reply. His first card, the three, wins, but his strangely disengaged demeanor, as though he is unconscious, causes concern in those around him, which increases as he bets his winnings on the seven and again wins. Hermann castigates the assembled company for seeming frightened, and calls for wine. Glass in hand, he sings, "What is our life? A game! Good and evil are only dreams!"—for him, life's purpose is to grasp the lucky moment. Hermann wishes to place another bet, but the card dealer, Chekalinsky, tells him to take what he has won, adding, "The Devil himself is playing alongside you!" Hermann retorts, "And if that were so, what's the harm in it?" Eletsky steps forward, despite attempts by the others to dissuade him, after Hermann asks for someone to play against. Chekalinsky once more deals. "My ace!" cries Hermann, showing the card he expects will win. But his card is not an ace—it is a queen: the queen of spades.

The ghost of the countess appears. Hermann asks it why it is laughing. He stabs himself, asks Eletsky's forgiveness, and then sees a vision of Liza whom he senses forgives him. He dies, and a prayer commending his soul to God is sung around him.

The Queen of Spades, composed in 1890, was premiered at the Mariinsky Theater on 19 December of that year, conducted by Nápravník. Its libretto and the accompanying music have often been considered ostentatiously operatic. The supernatural aspect of the original tale is strongly emphasized and broadened in the opera, as too is Hermann's madness. Furthermore, whereas in the short story the hero and heroine remain alive, their operatic counterparts both die. In fact, despite occasional melodramatic touches, most of the adaptations of Pushkin's narrative are well justified, and the music blends with them with singularly perceptive dramatic force.

When the ghost of the countess appears to Hermann in Pushkin's text, the fact that she comes shuffling along in her slippers to tell him the secret of the three cards adds to the likelihood that she is a manifestation of nothing more than the great amount of wine he had drunk to calm himself after her funeral. This had merely "excited his imagination even more."[1] In the opera, on the other hand, the ghost's entry is given grand, histrionic treatment, with a somewhat noisy orchestral climax as a way of trying to depict terror. Although the opera also allows the interpretation that the ghost is the product of Hermann's imaginings, this particular moment is disappointingly overblown in pure stage terms. This miscalculation is, nevertheless, subsumed by the buildup of dramatic tensions overall in the opera. So, by the end, two scenes later, when Hermann, in the gambling house, has declared his third card, but loses catastrophically nonetheless, and the ghost reappears, exacerbating his sense of horror, his stature has built to that of a genuinely tragic figure. In Pushkin's story, at the corresponding point, there is no ghost, but a much more dry and ironical treatment: Hermann thinks he sees the queen of spades screw up its eyes and grin, its face uncannily resembling that of the old countess (in the opera, the specter is laughing, the suggestion of which, therefore, clearly came from Pushkin). In both works there is a reference to the countess's corpse winking at Hermann at the funeral, although Pushkin treats this with characteristic humor. In his text the superstitious Hermann, who feels no remorse whatsoever, comes, cynically, to try to gain the deceased's forgiveness to ward off any future malign influence that she

might have on his life. He is so shocked when he sees her wink that he comically tumbles off the catafalque and crashes headlong to the floor. That incident does not occur in the opera, however, where, as we will see, the
winking corpse is portrayed in such a remarkably special musical context that
it enhances both the deceased countess and the terrified Hermann.

In both works it is the Count Saint-Germain who imparts the secret of
the three winning cards to the young countess. However, the specter who
appears to her subsequently, relating a dire prophecy, does not occur in
Pushkin, but only in the opera. Although undoubtedly "operatic" in the con-
ventional sense, this feature is far from gratuitous. It adds substantially to the
dramatic structure of the opera, firstly because the intervention of this spectral figure adds weight to Hermann's crazed perception that it is, finally,
malign Fate that propels him into confronting the countess in her bedchamber (Act 2 scene 2) and trying to extract the secret card formula. The "confirming" counterpart to that, as it were, is Liza's invitation to him (in the
preceding scene) to come, via a secret staircase leading initially into the
countess's bedroom, to her own room beyond, so that matters between her
beloved and her may be resolved. He is now convinced that Fate wills the
confrontation. Secondly, the countess's death from the fright of the debacle,
which culminates in Hermann's pointing a pistol at her, is given all the more
chilling stage effect through the audience's perception that she may be
thinking that Hermann is indeed the "third one" whom the apparition had
told her would come, to learn the three cards "by force"—which would
thereby cause her death. The other precondition stipulated in the augury,
that the bringer of her demise would be "ardently and passionately in love,"
is perhaps recalled to the countess when she hears Hermann beg her to
reveal the cards "if you have ever known the feeling of love"—which may
imply that he himself is currently bound up in some amorous involvement
(as in fact he is, with Liza). Although the last-quoted phrase does come, with
slight adaptation, from Pushkin (the corresponding fatal encounter between
Hermann and the countess in the short story),[2] its context is very different,
there being no supernatural prophecy at all in the original text. Pushkin's
countess dies simply and understandably because the frailty of her old age is
unable to withstand the shock of this stranger in her bedchamber threatening her with a pistol to learn the card formula.

The eventual insanity of the hero in Pushkin's tale is a far less important
aspect of it than the methodical charting of Hermann's mental breakdown
throughout the opera. The only unquestionable harbinger of Hermann's
mental collapse as devised by Pushkin (setting aside the wine-related vision
of the ghost) is the countess's corpse suddenly derisively smiling and winking at him at the funeral (whether one sees that as having really occurred in
some kind of supernatural manifestation, or as having been hallucinated by
the hero; if the former, it could well begin to unhinge him, and, if the latter, it

could mean his sanity was already giving way). This is economically referred to again at the end of the short story where, as we saw, it seems to Hermann that the card that had defeated him contorted its eyes and grinned, the features of the queen of spades resembling those of the deceased. In a pointedly brief conclusion appended to the final chapter, Pushkin informs us that Hermann has ended up insane, in an institution, constantly muttering, "Three, seven, ace! Three, seven, queen!" His madness is scarcely more than peripheral to Pushkin's plot. The same short appendix also tells us that Liza has gone on to marry a young man in the civil service. The mental disintegration of Hermann in the operatic adaptation will be assessed presently.

The opera's Liza, when she sees that she cannot save Hermann from his all-consuming gambling obsession, commits suicide. To make the deaths of both of the opera's principal protagonists more plausible, there are a number of other changes. Liza is here the countess's granddaughter, rather than, as in Pushkin, an orphan who has been taken into her care. Accordingly, when in the opera Hermann uses Liza as a means of reaching the old woman and unwittingly causes the latter's death, he has destroyed someone who is Liza's blood relative. That the man whom the heroine loves has done such a thing makes her prey to appallingly torn feelings, which might, if suddenly inverted upon herself at a moment of hopelessness, lead her to self-destruction.

In the short story, Hermann had no warm feelings whatsoever toward Liza, using her absolutely coldly and manipulatively. For example, he declares his love for her in a letter whose wording is copied verbatim from a German novel. In the opera, however, even though the hero indubitably uses the heroine as a pawn (although here he does not write her any letters), he not only loves Liza, but has a consuming possessive desire for her. That is aggravated by her being noble-born (which in Pushkin she is not), which places her above his social status and, accordingly, renders her unlikely to be attainable. It is this perilously insecure but passionate love, when combined with the compulsive need to gamble, that eventually unbalances Hermann's mind, making his death a natural outcome of the dramatic design of the opera. His stabbing himself would, beyond doubt, have been melodramatic and entirely unjustified if it had occurred at the end of Pushkin's original story, but having been invented as a conclusion to the opera, with its plot emphasis upon Hermann's mental instability and consequent vulnerability, it is both shocking and, in dramatic terms, absolutely right. The passions that his frail humanity has made him incapable of controlling engulf him.

Tchaikovsky articulated the dramatic structure of the music of *The Queen of Spades* through a complex application of compositional techniques, such that this is by far the most intricately designed of his operas. The most evident device is the very frequent and atmospheric use of a leitmotif representing the three winning cards, which becomes strongly associated both with Hermann's obsessive need to discover their identity, and his mental collapse. His growing compulsions and insanity are also delineated by a profoundly imaginative use of progressively deepening and thickening woodwind tone colors, a symbolic miring. In this work, several Glinkan procedures for depicting the supernatural, and generally evil forces, appear again: notably the whole-tone scale; harmony based upon it (prominently the augmented triad); and the use of distantly related chords which weaken the sense of key but are threaded onto a common pivot tone. Fate itself, however, is designated by descending diatonic scales (cf., the analysis, above, of *Eugene Onegin*).

The three-cards leitmotif is clearly foreshadowed in the opera's Prelude, and it is more obliquely hinted at as a fragment of the melody that accompanies Hermann onstage for his first appearance, in the opening scene. It eventually crystallizes, in its full form, to mark the first entrance of the countess and Liza, later in that same scene; even here, however, although it is clear that it is significant, the leitmotif has not yet been identified as a representation of the three cards. By the same token, the clothing of the melody in clarinet tone—two clarinets play it, in their dark-hued and evocative lowest region (the "chalumeau" register)—merely conveys a certain frisson, as befits the first appearance of the two women whose roles will intertwine with Hermann's with such devastating consequences. Perhaps because the countess, the heroine, and the hero form a sort of ill-fated triangle, revolving around the three cards as the means through which Hermann eventually feels he may deliver himself from his emotional impasse, the leitmotif is a symbolic fusion: three multiplied by three. A three-pitch motif (a descent of a semitone, F-E, and a leap of four steps to A) is restated a tone higher, then a tone higher again. Nine pitches form the complete leitmotif. The rising nature of the progression conveys a sense of hope, but its mechanistically sequential quality belies this. It actually represents false hope.

The slow formulation in Hermann's mind of the idea of learning the three cards is masterfully handled in the score. He by no means has his obsession from the start, nor even the thought itself of acquiring the countess's secret. Instead, circumstances and their musical depiction tighten around him, channeling him into the calamitous choice that he ultimately makes, unable, through his mind's instability, to withstand these pressures. The seeds of his tragedy are symbolized in the music that accompanies him the first time he walks onstage. A solo cello plays a theme containing a descending scale representing Fate, the final two tones of which (A and G) are followed by an upward leap of a fifth (to D).[3] Thus, Fate's insidious influence in the plot is adumbrated by its scale passing seamlessly into a motif that is relatable to the three-cards leitmotif (whose basic unit is similar to the specified tones in the preceding sentence). Moreover, this cello melody can retrospectively be seen as having voiced the emotional undercurrent in Hermann's mind for, as he appears, "pensive [and] somber" according to the stage direction, he denies to his companion, Tomsky, that anything is the matter with him. He does not actually sing the melody; only the cello has it. It then passes to a solo bassoon, and still Hermann does not sing it, but reveals that there is great uncertainty in his life now. Suddenly, however, after Hermann at last discloses that he is in love and is asked with whom, he does sing, to the melody that the cello and bassoon had played, "I do not know her name, and cannot find out, not wishing to call her by an earthly name." He soon adds (in a recitative) that she is "noble-born and cannot belong to me!" The extent of Hermann's emotional pain in his longing for this unreachable woman is thus movingly conveyed by his reluctance in revealing it, for he only actually sings the melody that embodies that longing the third time we hear it in the opera.

When Tomsky attempts to console Hermann by opining that the woman he longs for reciprocates that feeling, he concedes this to be a "comforting doubt" that lessens the torment in his soul. Hermann's rhetorical, suicidal threat—that only death would remain to him should he discover that he is fated never to have his beloved—is then dramatically put in focus by the arrival of his unwitting nemesis, Prince Eletsky. Eletsky (who does not appear, and has no counterpart, in Pushkin's story, his role in the opera being entirely connected with Liza's elevation, in the libretto, to the nobility)[4] is betrothed to the beloved whom Hermann feels himself denied because of her social status, that same status that grants the prince easier access. Ominously, as a portent whose significance will take a long time to become apparent, the point at which Eletsky, by gesture, identifies to whom he is engaged—the arrival onstage of Liza (in the company of the countess)—brings with it not only the three-cards leitmotif in its distinctive clarinet coloring but also a pounding accompaniment, on the horns, transferring to clarinets and bassoons, whose frantic dotted rhythm will recur when Hermann at last plays the first of the three cards in the gambling house at the end of the opera. By then, that hectic rhythm asserts the crazed determination with which he engages in gambling with the card formula. It is notable also that here, at the first entry of the two women, there is another musical augury, as heightening the pulsating accompaniment there appear two rushing scalar ascents, partly based on the whole-tone system,[5] as Hermann twice exclaims, "O, God!" at the realization that Liza is Eletsky's fiancée. This foreshadows the use of the whole-tone scale in its typical, Glinkan, *descending* form when the countess's ghost appears to Hermann in Act 3 scene 1.

During exchanges between the countess and Tomsky in which, alarmed at the sight of his companion, she asks who Hermann is, there appears, emphasizing her anxiety, the augmented triad, a harmonic reference to the fleeting whole-tone scales that have just underlined Hermann's anguish (and also to the later whole-tone scale accompanying the ghost of the countess). Furthermore, the three-cards leitmotif now proliferates, saturating the orchestral texture and displaying many dissonant intervallic leaps, notably tritones, symbolizing diabolical influence.[6] Then, the first distinct hint that the leitmotif is connected with cards and gambling arises. Having escorted the countess to a distance, Tomsky returns. While Hermann's companions, Surin and Chekalinsky, speak derisively of her, Hermann's theme of longing for the unreachable beloved sounds in the background, on violas, as he himself sits, silently sunk in reflection. As the melody's second phrase is ending, the three-cards leitmotif is suddenly and surreptitiously added to it, on a single clarinet, in chalumeau register. Seeming like an interruption of Hermann's train of thought, the leitmotif again makes use of the tritone, and occurs immediately after Tomsky utters the words:"The Queen of Spades," the nickname he states the countess had been given. Thus, the name of a playing card, the very one that will cause Hermann's downfall, has been joined both with the countess and with Hermann's melody of longing for the unattainable beloved. The use of low-register clarinet tone furthers the impression of an as yet undefined link between Hermann, his desired one, and the woman with whom she first walked onstage.

A clarification of the significance of the three-cards leitmotif comes at its fresh occurrence while Tomsky sings that the countess, as an adored young beauty in Paris, was nevertheless only really interested in cards: "Throughout each night [she] gambled." Then Tomsky commences his ballad. Only now may we fully discern that the leitmotif, which we have already heard repeatedly in this opening scene, relates to three cards. "One day," he begins, "at Versailles" the countess lost everything she had at the gambling table. He reveals that she had then whispered, "O God, I could win everything back if I only had enough money again to bet on"— underpinning those words, the orchestra plays the three-cards leitmotif—"three cards, three cards, three cards!" Underpinning the last-quoted words comes almost nothing. Tomsky sings them almost entirely unaccompanied. Although they retrospectively give verbal definition to the leitmotif, that leitmotif itself here falls silent. At the very point that definition arises, it points simultaneously toward a new connection, for it is a stroke of Tchaikovsky's genius that Tomsky sings "three cards, three cards, three cards" to Hermann's melody of longing for the unreachable beloved, presented in a new rhythm. So, the countess's wish, through a bet on three cards, to regain all the money she had lost is provocatively entangled with the theme that represents Hermann's wish to reach the beloved who he felt was unattainable anyway, and who now seems lost because of her betrothal to Eletsky. Loss, and a desire to regain, form the common threads. The musical symbolism itself appears to point Hermann in the direction of gambling, as a hinted means of regaining Liza. It is unlikely, however, that any deliberate irony on Tomsky's part is intended; Hermann's friend seems, rather, to be *unconsciously* recalling the melody that Hermann had sung (for the different rhythm gives it a quite contrasted aspect).[7]

The juxtaposition of the three-cards leitmotif and the rhythmically altered permutation of Hermann's theme sung to the thrice-stated "three cards" is then repeated as Tomsky tells how Count Saint-Germain offered the countess the winning formula of the cards, and it is stated for the third time as he concludes with the apparition's prophecy of the countess dying after the third man comes to her, in a deeply enamored state, demanding, by force, to learn the secret cards. As Tomsky narrates the words of the countess, Saint-Germain, and the specter, augmented triads appear in the accompaniment of the three-cards leitmotif on each occasion. Thus, the use of the same harmony that had underlined the countess's anxious reaction to Hermann earlier in the scene recurs in that part of the unfolding story where we first learn of the existence of the ultimately tragically significant three-cards secret, with its implications for the countess's death. Furthermore, the role of the supernatural, as expressed with the appearance of the apparition, is also conveyed by the augmented triad.

As a storm gathers in the distance, Chekalinsky mocks the impecunious Hermann with the proposition that he now has an excellent opportunity, through the card formula, to gamble without money. Surin joins in the taunt, he and Chekalinsky reiterating most of the specter's words of warning to the young countess. The storm that breaks out in Hermann's heart, however, is not yet to do with acquiring the card secret, for as the other characters disperse and Hermann is left alone to make a declaration to the tempest around him, he first repeats the apparition's words as Tomsky had related them in full, but then dismisses any idea of the cards being of use to him, as he feels his whole world is now destroyed. The specter's declaration, both as quoted by Chekalinsky and Surin on the one hand, and Hermann on the other, is underlain by a resurgence of the three-cards leitmotif in its harmonization employing augmented triads. Between these two passages come the following events: A forceful clap of thunder rings out, also to the orchestral accompaniment of the augmented triad, and this chord very effectively persists into the start of a brief chorus of strollers, taken unawares by the storm. Nature's rage, the tempest, touches upon Hermann's personal rage through the functioning, it seems, of the supernatural, as betokened by this distinctive, intertwining link of harmony.

At the end of the strollers' chorus, as they rush to shelter from the storm, Hermann's theme of longing for the unreachable beloved sounds, without his singing it, on chalumeau-register clarinets in unison with bassoons. His desired one might be his shelter, if only the attaining of her would not involve an inevitable storm. The same dark clarinet timbre that had attended Liza and the countess when they had first appeared, and which had returned for the enunciation of the latter's sobriquet "The Queen of Spades," is now thickened with bassoon tone as Hermann silently broods upon the intensification of his problems arising from the involvement of Eletsky with Liza. As

Hermann then declares of the secret cards, "O, what's in them for me! Even if I would possess them! My whole world is crushed now," the melody of yearning for the unattainable beloved is played again, in the background, by the same woodwinds that have just rendered it. That instrumental coloring will appear with an extra accretion of woodwind parts when, in the next scene, Hermann acts on the impulse which he now reveals at the end of the first scene, and which, standing alone, he solemnly proclaims to the storm around him, like a man teetering on the edge of insanity: "While I live, I'll not give her up [to Prince Eletsky]. . . . Mine shall she be, mine, mine, or I'll die!"

"O listen, night!" sings Liza, alone in her room, in Act 1 scene 2. She confides to it her dark, secret love of someone, which has her as though captive to him. Here some of the opera's most expressive and original music unfolds. A pattern of hushed, rustling string figuration arises, not quite like anything elsewhere in Tchaikovsky's output, and it is interspersed with rich harp arpeggios, denoting Liza's rapturous but also troubled excitement. At the culmination of this passage, Hermann suddenly appears in the doors of the balcony. He is accompanied by a tumid and deliberately ugly sound: Most of the woodwind section (i.e., all of the following: flutes, oboes, clarinets, and bassoons) play a single, prolonged pitch, in unison (the E flat above middle C). That is a gross intensification of tone color, very effectively emphasizing the exaggerated, rash nature of Hermann's action in acquainting himself with his beloved in this way, for this is their first meeting. Beneath the sustained E flat, the strings play successive chords that gradually loosen any sense of key, but that all share that tone as a pivot. Tchaikovsky's resumption of this Glinkan device not only conveys its usual supernatural connotations (there is a subliminal hint at the opera's spectral subtext, simply because this type of musical structure had been adopted by Glinka's successors as a way of denoting the preternatural), but also embodies the emotional ambivalence of the hero and heroine. The undermining of tonality represents, at the deepest level, their anxiety that love might not succeed, and also Liza's shameful sense that her secret love of Hermann undermines the established rule of order as shown in her betrothal to another man. The long-held pivotal pitch carries an implication of their wish for their love to last, against everything that would buffet it. Among the chords beneath the pivot is an augmented triad, whose insidious presence at this juncture of Hermann and Liza's first meeting carries reminiscences from the opening scene, of anxiety and the aura of the supernatural specifically surrounding the three cards.

Hermann's passionate declaration to Liza of his feelings for her is interrupted by the arrival of the irate countess, disturbed by the noise from Liza's room. After she knocks at the door and demands to be let in, the three-cards leitmotif, on clarinets, occurs profusely, displaying many reiterated demonic tritone leaps, which relates back to the same instrumental setting for the leit-motif's tritonal rendition at mention of her gambling nickname in the pre-ceding scene (though here the clarinets play very little in their chalumeau register, passing quickly into their upper regions).

This dissonant fruition at the sudden emergence of the countess stands for an evil enticement to Hermann—like the intercession of some fateful external force, expressed only in terms of the orchestral accompaniment—to gain knowledge of the secret cards. After she has reprimanded Liza and departed, and Hermann, previously hidden, can now articulate his thoughts, his reaction is first to sing a paraphrase of the specter's prophecy (while the cards' leitmotif again sounds in the background), and then to exclaim, "The coldness of the grave has blown around me! O terrible apparition, death, I do not want you!" He delivers those words while a tremolo is played by chalumeau-register clarinets, that timbre therefore gaining an association with the concept of death itself.

Moreover, he sings "apparition, death" to a motif—D falling by step to C, followed by an upward leap of a fifth to G—which echoes the basic unit of the three-cards leitmotif, and the last of these pitches, G, setting "death," forms an overlap, as it is the first tone of a Fate-evoking scalar descent through the subsequent words, "I do not want you!" This reverses the struc-ture we observed in Hermann's melody of longing for the unreachable beloved, where a Fate-symbolizing scale came first, followed by a three-pitch motif evoking the cards' leitmotif. However, there is an element that remains the same, namely the use of an overlap, for that earlier melody had also knit-ted together the transition between the scale and the three-pitch motif. As we saw, two pitches there formed the region of the fusing-together. Now, just one pitch does so. By the subtlest possible means, Tchaikovsky indicates, just as Hermann seems to be experiencing the greatest aversion to any inter-est in the secret cards, that predestination is operating immutably—even though it has dwindled to the smallest degree of perceptibility—and may indeed trap him into trying to learn them. Whether Fate or the card formula itself is hinted at first is immaterial; they are inextricably linked, the music appears to say. This finely judged compositional treatment is comparable to that revealed in Tomsky's ballad.

Hermann goes on to explain his attitude toward death, which had seemed to him, merely a few moments before, to be salvation, but which now seems, in the light of Liza's having revealed the dawn of happiness to him, to be frightening. Indeed, just before the countess's interruption, Liza had wept at his confession of love and when he had taken her hand she had not drawn it away.

The net of circumstances tightens around the increasingly vulnerable Hermann in the following scene, that which opens Act 2, and whose setting, a masked ball, is masterly as backdrop to his progressive unhinging. Nothing can be judged at face value when those around one wear masks, and the rational thinking that maintains the individual at the level of sanity may seem undermined when all around him is ambiguous. Yet there is an even graver ambiguity—that within Hermann himself—for the means by which he will aim to secure his love are self-defeating. As a paradoxical symbol of his inability to see the fatally threatening emotional cleavage within him, Hermann himself, in the midst of the masquerade, does not actually wear a mask. His involuted psychological predicament is deftly contrasted with the plain allegory of the pastoral divertissement that is put on for the ball's guests, in which the sincere shepherdess, Prilepa, is not deflected from her true love for the penniless shepherd, Milovzor, by the wealthy Zlatogor's vain enticement of her with his riches. Hermann's dilemma might simply be seen as this: If love is pure, it needs nothing secondary to secure it. That is why Zlatogor's offer of wealth to win Prilepa is spurious, for that very offer implies he does not love her but merely seeks to add her, as a resplendent human object, to the glittering jewels that are already part of his riches. As Hermann is unfortunate enough, as a commoner, to be below Liza's social rank as an aristocrat, and seeks the acquisition of great wealth as a substitute for such high social status, that solution itself is self-negating. It puts him in an intolerable and indeed potentially sanity-threatening double bind: If he can only present himself to her as a valid partner by becoming wealthy, it means that he himself, unadorned, is unworthy. To try to prove his love, he must demean it.

It is, moreover, deeply ironic that when, in Act 3 scene 2, Hermann's sanity finally collapses and his raw humanity is at its most unadorned, Liza nevertheless holds true to him, wishing him to run away with her so she can save him. The need he had persuaded himself of, to win her through wealth, turns out to be utterly irrelevant, but he cannot now grasp this, because his rationality has been wrecked, and he pushes her away, no longer capable even of recognizing who she is, and she, confounded, commits suicide. In a sense, the slippery path toward that catastrophe begins here in Act 2 scene 1, for it is here that we discover his deranged notion of going to the countess to learn the secret card combination. We do not, however, learn of it first from Hermann himself; the revelation comes from Surin, who does not state when he came to know of Hermann's intention, restricting himself, during a conversation with Chekalinsky and Tomsky, merely to observing that Hermann is "distracted—with what, do you think, with what? The hope of discovering the three cards. . . . He told me himself."

That "distracted" hope, which can be deemed so as it is yet to be resolved, begins to solidify into an actual intention, on either side of the sincere-shepherdess interlude. Fueling Hermann's descent into pursuing that intention are two contradistinct influences upon him: one loving, namely the increasingly close approaches to him of Liza, and the other mischievous, that is, the increasingly irresponsible taunting of him by Surin (joined initially by Chekalinsky) as to whether or not he is the third one, referred to in the spectral prophecy, who will extract the card secret and cause the countess's death. Hermann's ambivalent love, which draws him painfully toward Liza, also lessens his resistance to Surin and Chekalinsky's taunts, for their destructive suggestions may seem genuinely to show how his beloved might be captured and the ambivalence surrounding her thus vanquished. The painful psychological struggle is deftly encapsulated in a circular shape in the events in the libretto, betokening the risk that Hermann may simply expend enormous effort to end up where he started, with an ambivalence that cannot be resolved. The circle begins with Liza's note to Hermann (which he reads aloud) asking to meet him after the performance (of the pastoral interlude). Love beckons, therefore—a deeply yearned for but tragically unreachable love. The next point on the circle comes with an enticement to tragically reachable self-destruction: Surin and Chekalinsky steal up to Hermann and whisper, "Are you not the third one who, passionately loving, will come to learn from [the countess] the three cards. . .?" As they disappear into the crowd before he can see who they are, one can understand the anxious thoughts he then mutters to himself, that he may have gone mad. Now comes the third point on the circle, the heart of the matter: the allegory presented in "The Shepherdess's Sincerity" entertainment, of the uncomplicated nature of pure love (as opposed to Hermann's increasingly tortuous moral dilemma).

The third point on the circle having passed with the ending of the pastorale, two further points are now reached, which seem to reverse the order of the first two. There now comes a taunting event followed by one portending the fruition of love. Surin, masked, takes advantage of the fortuitous circumstance of the countess and Hermann coming face to face with each other, after the pastoral entertainment's conclusion, to exclaim, "Look, your mistress!" He then, once again, hides, to add to the effect of the ridicule. This is a particularly hazardous moment for further taunting to occur, for just after the pastorale and just before finding himself in front of the countess, the thought had come into Hermann's head concerning his possible connection with the ardently and passionately loving man cited in the apparition's prophecy: "Surely I am in love [i.e., with Liza]? Of course . . . yes!" That dangerous perception immediately brings from the orchestra a brief outburst in response, containing an augmented triad,[8] a warning, yet again, of the destructive influence of the supernatural, occurring at the very moment that Hermann turns and sees the countess. As they both shudder and stare at each other, there is an emotive, yet subtle resurgence of an accompanimental pattern that had occurred at a deeply significant juncture of the opera's opening scene, the point at which Hermann had learned that Liza was betrothed to Eletsky. When Liza had walked onstage, with the countess, to be identified by the prince as his bride-to-be, the horns had emitted a loud and insistent accompaniment in rapid dotted rhythm, which had then passed onto bassoons in combination with this opera's baleful instrumental harbingers, the clarinets. That had been the musical depiction of the moment at which Hermann's world had irrevocably changed. The clarinets and a bassoon now bring back the dotted-rhythm accompaniment, as though to represent thoughts brewing in Hermann's mind in connection with that earlier event; the implication is of his pondering a way to circumvent the catastrophe of losing Liza to Eletsky—and, indeed, of his deliberations occurring while he is staring into the eyes of the countess, the woman who may hold the very secret he needs. Surin's destructive ridiculing of Hermann occurs while the dotted-rhythm accompaniment is restated (on bassoons and a horn) one octave lower, as of a descent into even greater danger.

Indeed, this provokes from Hermann an exclamation of distress, while the orchestra, in the background, again invokes music from a decisive event earlier in the opera. He declares that he cannot tell if the voice he has just heard is of demonic or human origin. During this, the orchestral strings build up an accompanying structure of chords shifting around a pitch they hold in common, and that pivot tone (an E) is sustained by the woodwinds, with increasingly thickening timbre, an oboe presently being joined at the unison by, first, two flutes, then a clarinet. This relates back to the even more dense woodwind unison that had marked Hermann's reckless first meeting with Liza (Act 1 scene 2), when he appeared on the balcony to her room. Indeed, the two scenes are both dramatically and musically cognate. In the earlier one, Hermann had been an intruder at the countess's home, having come, uninvited, to acquaint himself with her granddaughter and discover if she loves him. In the later one, he is in the general context of contemplating an even more foolhardy approach, at some time, to the countess herself, to attempt to discover a putative secret that he knows of only through Tomsky's lurid story about it, and which might not, in fact, even exist. Similar Glinkan musical methods are employed, in both instances, to depict supernatural workings, which are more explicit in the masked ball, with Hermann's anxiety that the voice he has heard may be that of a demon (whereas they were only implicit, as we saw, in the balcony encounter).

While Hermann and Liza, in the original event, had looked silently at each other, and the strings had played a series of chords that, although hooked onto a common pitch, had strayed far from a sense of key, Hermann and the Countess now stare silently at each other, Surin utters his diabolical taunt, and the pivotally shifting string harmonies stay broadly, if a little ambivalently, within the system of tonality, alternating between the keys of A minor and C major, with a small amount of chromaticism,[9] and then passing on to E minor for Hermann's cry: "Curse it!" The maintaining of a basis in key structure seems to indicate that circumstances are solidifying around

Hermann and, whether it be through supernatural forces or his diminishing sanity or both, his path is becoming increasingly fixed, despite his anxieties which, indeed, seem increasingly immaterial by this point.

Now, at the height of his distress, Liza appears. This should herald hope. It actually places him, albeit in an entirely different and therefore less clear way, in the same irresolvable torment. The hand of a great operatic master is revealed in the simple way in which Tchaikovsky points to this. At the moment when Liza enters, in a mask, the whole significance of this is entrusted to an accompanimental figuration of rapid notes on an entirely unpropitious instrument: the clarinet. Furthermore, just as in the case of the clarinet providing a musical tag after Tomsky's mention of the countess's nickname, "The Queen of Spades," in his ballad, so too here, no other instruments are playing. In both instances the clarinet, without any accompaniment whatsoever, holds the thread of the opera. Whatever is to ensue, it secures it—it is the stepping-stone over which events will pass.

Now comes the fatal turning point in Hermann's fortunes. Liza wishes him to come to her tomorrow, giving him the key to the secret door of the countess's garden so he may ascend a staircase, pass through the bedroom of the old woman—who will not be there—and on into her own room. They "must settle everything!" and she vows she will belong to him alone. But that vow, which makes things seem, after all, as though they are going his way, also completes the too-perfect symmetry of events that began with Liza's note to him earlier in the scene. The cultivating of love, the taunt, the allegory of reachable love, the taunt, and the cultivating of love have now come back in a circle. Hermann's suppressed self-destructiveness then expresses itself in over-confidence. He demands that they meet later today, not tomorrow. She agrees to that and departs. Now he feels that events themselves are leading him to the countess and her secret. Fate, he believes, will have it so. The die is cast, for he has abandoned free will.

Perhaps Tchaikovsky's operatic genius never expressed itself more momentously than in the scene that follows. In Act 2 scene 2, despite some tormenting doubts, Hermann advances with reckless tenacity to confront the countess, and the ebb and flow of their conflicting emotions is pervasively revealed in the music. The subdued start to the scene establishes a static atmosphere, as a protracted stretch of music, forty-eight measures in length, unfolds—without any contribution at all from other instrumental families—on the strings, *con sordini* (i.e., all the stringed instruments carry a muting device to remove the warmth of their sound), before there is any notable change in the mood of the music. When that change comes, it is startling, for the pure but deadened string tone is suddenly intruded upon by a phrase on the lower woodwinds; although dark in timbre itself, this provides paradoxical relief after such an expanse of greyness, and it very effectively underlines Hermann's exclamation, "So, it is decided, I'll find out the secret from the old woman!"[10]

It is in this scene that the bass clarinet makes its first appearance in the opera. Its symbolism is clear—an intensification of all the anxious associations and ill augury that have attended its sister, the standard orchestral clarinet, achieved simply through the same timbre being deepened in pitch. Indeed, the bass clarinet is to be Hermann's companion in his madness (a usage of a woodwind instrument derived, as we saw in regard to *Mazeppa*, from early nineteenth-century Italian opera) attending him in his crazed act of confronting the countess in the present scene, and then, finally, confirming his madness, in his meeting with Liza, two scenes hence. The instrument makes its very first sounds while Hermann finds himself immovable with fascination in front of a portrait of the countess when young, radiant with her erstwhile beauty as "The Muscovite Venus." He broods on Fate linking him to her in a way that will cause one of them to precipitate the other's death, and he looks on her image and hates "but cannot look enough." Now the bass clarinet surreptitiously arises, peering into the music for the first time as though through a mask, for its timbre is hidden by being mixed at the unison with two bassoons (with whose tone color it blends exceptionally well) as all these instruments, with double basses at the octave beneath lessening the bass clarinet's prominence still further, sound the three-cards leitmotif.

Then Hermann sings, "I would like to run away, but lack the strength." His inability to apply free will is again underlined. The subtle nature of the use of the bass clarinet shows its double-edged purpose. It is like an extension into the orchestra of the persona of Surin, ostensibly a companion and yet issuing destructive taunts from behind a mask, the only difference being that it is hidden in aural rather than physical terms. Tchaikovsky's strategy here seems to be to bring in the bass clarinet repeatedly in the background, as of its being something insidious, until it stands fully revealed when Hermann passes the point of no return. Its role, in other words, is in almost complete contrast to that of the woodwind instruments and, even more notably, the solo violin that act as Maria's companions in her decline into insanity in *Mazeppa*. There, the heroine's mental collapse brought the support of a whole sympathetic succession of solo instruments; here, the hero has a decidedly ambivalent and indeed mocking companion in the form of the bass clarinet. That, of course, reflects their different circumstances, for Maria is more genuinely hapless than Hermann, who is overcome, finally, by his greed.

Before the bass clarinet emerges fully, it makes further appearances in the background in, for example, Liza's conversation with her servant Masha, and the countess's monologue—as Hermann hides, waiting for his moment to approach her. Masha senses, through her mistress's pallor, that something is wrong and Liza concedes that "he" (i.e., Hermann) may already be here and that she is acting on his orders. After she has added that she has become the "obedient, true slave" of the one whom Fate has sent her, an acknowledgment that she has, indeed, like Hermann, given up free will (albeit temporarily, whereas her beloved has entirely lost his grip on it), the bass clarinet creeps into the orchestral texture as she and Masha depart, playing a brief, chromatically ascending scale, while beneath and above it the string section reprises part of the introductory music to the chorus of the countess's hangers-on and maids (who had sung earlier and who now sing again, providing the countess with her last-ever experience of nonthreatening human companionship, much though she does not want to have anything to do with them). When the Countess sings that she has "had enough of this world," she enunciates a descending scale of six steps, a back-reference filled with dramatic irony, for it relates both to Hermann's melody of longing for the unreachable beloved, from the opera's opening scene, and to Tomsky's melody as he sang, in his ballad, of the countess's obsession with three cards, both of which, as we saw, contained a six-degree descent. She sings her phrase almost completely without any accompaniment, a leanness of presentation that (as on so many occasions in this opera, either as concerns a solo instrument or voice) shows it is of fundamental significance. She presently sings a nostalgic reminiscence (putatively of her youthful years) of an aria from Grétry's opera *Richard Cœur-de-Lion*—an anachronism, however, as that work was in fact premiered in 1784, making it too late to be anything other than a part of her maturity or old age. Its words are a further, intense irony in view of what the audience knows of Hermann's intentions toward her. It begins: "Je crains de lui parler la nuit, j'écoute trop tout ce qu'il dit" ("I fear talking to him at night, I hear all too well everything he says"). After singing it, she appears suddenly to rouse herself from her reverie of reminiscing and contemptuously orders her entourage out. Then, as she falls asleep, the bass clarinet has its moment of greatest prominence so far. Its sister instrument, the clarinet, echoes the six-step scalar descent that the countess had earlier sung to express her being weary with the world, and this, in its turn, is echoed by the bass clarinet beneath, thrown into relief by a sustained tone on a single bassoon.

But the bass clarinet's ascent into primacy only comes at the opera's turning point, for after the countess drifts into sleep, repeating her Grétry aria, there comes a brief, dead calm at the start of the scene's finale. Above divided cellos, marked to play at the merest whisper, the bass clarinet now carries, without help from any other instrument and without merely engaging in an echo, the opera's most fraught emblem: the leitmotif of the three cards. Seconds later, Hermann stands in front of the countess, and she awakens in dumb terror.

"Don't be afraid! For God's sake don't be afraid!" he begs. Now the orchestra's woodwind section comes into its own in portraying the surrealistic horror of the situation. A rapid clarinet arpeggio acts as catalyst to an outburst of mocking acciaccaturas, notes of extremely brief duration, from the bassoons and the remaining clarinet. "I will not cause you any harm!" declares Hermann, and the two clarinets enter into an obsessional and turbulent interchange with each other, their flurry of alternating arpeggios indicating the feverish anxiety both of Hermann as he advances himself in a pointless and disastrous situation, and the countess in being confronted by this crazed interloper. The sinister tone of the bass clarinet then returns to deliver the leitmotif of the cards after Hermann's statement, "You know three cards," and then again after he adds: "For whom must you keep your secret?"

Such an accretion of clarinet timbre, both of the standard instrument and its bass counterpart, is ominous indeed. Furthermore, the bass clarinet then reverts to its earlier, covert, role, which is perhaps all the more chilling after having shown its full face. It blends into the midst of an accompaniment, which develops on the strings and wind instruments, to Hermann's plea to the countess to reveal her secret to him if ever she has "known the feeling of love."

Finally, exasperated, he threatens her with the pistol. As she responds to him by nodding her head, raising her hands so as to shield herself from being shot, and then dropping down dead of fright, a clarinet arpeggio once again ushers in a derisory burst of bassoon and clarinet acciaccaturas, and the frenetic exchange of arpeggios between the two clarinets also recurs. These sounds, which had created such a striking effect when Hermann begged her, for the Almighty's sake, not to be frightened and when he had assured her he would not harm her, were in fact a portent that she had every reason to be afraid, and that he would hurt her, and they now return to confirm it. Just as no shot has actually been fired by Hermann, so too the Countess has withheld something. It is not just that she has not revealed the secret cards—she has not even, in the whole of their encounter, uttered a single word. Hermann's fractured sanity has been granted no reprieve, neither affirmation nor denial of the existence of the card secret that has so tormented him.

Now his lover enters. So, too, has a new reality entered, one engendered by him. He must face its emotional consequences, consequences that may indeed lead to the final destruction of his sanity. Liza is horrified at what he has done, denounces him and orders him out.

Alone in his room at the barracks at the start of the following Act, he faces his next ordeal. Hope tears him in opposite directions with the reading of a letter from Liza. As he recites it, his dependably grim comrade, the bass clarinet, plays entirely unaccompanied in the background, quite high in its compass at first, but winding lower and lower until, after he finishes reading, it reaches its lowest pitch. That precedes his exclamation, "Poor girl!"—but he is no less wretched than her; indeed he declares he has lured her into an abyss with him. Her note had revealed her willingness to forgive him, her belief that he did not wish to cause her grandmother's death, but also an offer to him to put her mind at rest by coming to meet her on the embankment by midnight. If he does not do so, she will have to believe the worst. His instrumental companion had paid him a curiously ironical favor by digging deeper and deeper into its range while he read, for the hopelessness that that symbolizes matches the despair of his situation. He cannot be true to his lover and disavow the truth of his culpability for the countess's death.

Now he hopes for a little oblivion by falling asleep. Even here there lurks a torment, for as he seems to doze, he is plagued by memories of the countess's funeral. He suddenly stands up in a fright, and believes he can hear, once again, the sound of the choir at her obsequies. In a moment that matches the dramatic acumen of the bedchamber scene, Tchaikovsky employs an adaptation of an authentic Russian Orthodox chant at this point: "I pour out my prayer to the Lord," a plea for redemption from evil, which an offstage choir sings while Hermann, forlorn in the foreground, delivers disjointed snatches of recitative.

There are broader liturgical references here too. Although most of what Hermann is singing is broken, truncated, interspersed with many brief silences to depict his moral anguish and his paranoid anxiety as to whether what he hears is a funereal choir or just the howling of the wind, nevertheless his vocal line proceeds also in a way that reveals a liturgical root. Much of his part involves the frequent repetition of a pitch, as for example when he sings of his visions, "And there too is the church, and the crowd and the candles," each syllable of which is set to the tone G. The intensity of such repetition evokes the devotional and exhortatory singing of a Russian Orthodox priest,[11] an immense irony in view of Hermann's guilt for having (albeit unintentionally) caused the countess's death. Yet the falsity of his outlook, as he still clings, with quasi-religious fervor, to the hope of acquiring earthly wealth no matter what, is belied by the repeated intercession of short silences in his singing—continuity is confounded by the innate untenability of his position. All of that mortal angst is vitiated by the unbroken continuity of the church choir's sustained harmonies in the background. At this point Hermann gains dignity precisely through his human vulnerability, the ease with which he has succumbed to sin, for his frailties and the musical thinness of what he sings are rendered null by the encompassing breadth of the surrounding choral harmony, a representation of God's embracing love itself. Whether Tchaikovsky meant that consciously or not, it can be clearly discerned, and it counterbalances the dark undercurrent of the story—even Hermann's recollection, which comes to him just after the choir temporarily stops singing, of the dead countess having winked at him at the funeral seems mere grotesquerie in the light of what has just been revealed, for the old lady's appalling death itself is subsumed within the Almighty's overall purpose.

These liturgical moments—compounded by a brief return of the choir, in a plea to God to grant the deceased eternal life, in the midst of which Hermann orders his terrible vision away—will reach forward in a great, life-affirming arch to another such moment at the opera's close.

A knocking at the window begins and baleful statements of the three-cards leitmotif, cast in the colors of the clarinet, ensue. The ghost of the countess enters, and while a clarinet sounds a spectral whole-tone scale, she tells Hermann that the three, the seven, and the ace will win in succession, provided that he save and marry Liza. Now he has his secret.

The orchestral prelude to Act 3 scene 2 builds up an impressive textural thickness to depict the emotional mire of the heroine's predicament, with which the textural simplicity of her arioso, which follows it immediately, will no less impressively contrast. The woodwinds symbolically reprise the use of heavily compounded unisons that had marked her first, fateful meeting with her lover, in Act 1 scene 2. The improbable hopefulness of that moment, as Hermann stood on the balcony of her room, about to declare his passion for her, will now play itself out in hopelessness. Accordingly, flutes, oboes, and clarinets all join in a turgid unison to present the melody of this orchestral introduction, and the line is then further thickened by the addition of the bass clarinet and a bassoon. That particularly intense unison is established just as the curtain rises to reveal the scene that will frame Liza's tragedy, and the expressive sense of overstatement is palpable. By the Winter Canal at night, the heroine starts her arioso by singing that she is "weary of grief." Now we are faced not with the convolutedness of her situation but with the direct simplicity of her human emotions. Her words are supported by the simple homogeneity and warmth of the string section with its uniformity of tone-color rather than a labored spectrum of woodwind timbres. Her melody itself, as Garden points out, recalls the general style of Susanin's great aria "They guess the truth" in Glinka's first opera. Furthermore, the dramatic circumstances are comparable, as both Susanin and Liza will shortly die—the former through the overwhelming force of his captors, the latter through being overwhelmed by events and her split emotions. She becomes very much the suffering Russian woman, for folk style is at the root of her melody as it was of that of Glinka's hero,[12] and the sorrow of an individual is therefore, once again, magnified by alignment with a nation. That, indeed, releases the catharsis, with an element both of microcosm and macrocosm making a unity. This will, arguably, make Liza's death seem somewhat less shocking, for we have been subliminally alerted to the archetypal aspect of her suffering. Shocking it nevertheless remains.

The cruel twist comes with Liza's brief reunion with her lover, whose insanity then reveals itself for the first time beyond any doubt. As the defining revelation of his madness, it could hardly be more adroitly judged in dramatic terms. He interrupts their love-duet to ask if she is ready to run away with him. She asks where to, and adds she will go with him "even to the ends of the earth!" And then her emotional world starts to collapse, for he replies, "Run where? Where? To the gambling house!" The instrumental malefactor that had dogged his steps in the countess's bedchamber, the bass clarinet, now confirms he has gone mad, with obsessive repetitions of a six-tone descending scale while he sings, "There piles of gold are lying and to me, me alone do they belong!" Each one of those six pitches is set to the same rhythmic value,[13] and this gives the feel of a featureless landscape, as befits Hermann's mind having irrevocably lost its way. Moreover, the motif overall is a perfectly distilled symbol of the unbearable pressures in his life that have caused his mental collapse, for its melodic shape recalls the six-tone scalar descent that had featured both in his theme of longing for the unreachable beloved, which had accompanied our very first sight of him in the opera, and the melody in which Tomsky had recounted the young countess's lust for the chance to bet on three cards.[14] It is caught halfway between the opposite poles of attraction of love and gambling.

Fruition of that love disappears now. When Liza, despite her attempts to bring Hermann round, can see he is beyond hope, she ends her own hope by ending her life. It is a tragic and deeply moving display of empathy. A wretched and abominable hope still exists in Hermann, however: that of satiating the lust for gambling. He still lives, but his end is near.

In the final scene, with Liza's bereaved fiancé present and looking for vengeance, Hermann tries his luck at the gambling house. Tchaikovsky develops, at this point, material that has been employed with the most determined repetition in the course of the opera, along with material that has been encountered briefly and in only three previous locations: the Overture,[15] the very first scene, and Act 2 scene 1. He melds the dramatically oversuffused with the faintly remembered, another unity of macrocosm and microcosm, and another instance of this work's striking sense of the appropriate gesture at the appropriate moment, for this abiding unity prepares for the opera's closure. The leitmotif of the three cards is, naturally, the skillfully over-used element; the under-used one is the simple but forceful dotted-rhythm accompaniment that had set Eletsky's identification of Liza as his bride-to-be, who was then walking onstage for the first time, along with her grandmother, to Hermann's mortal discomfiture, and which had set in train the opera's sequence of events. This music had reappeared for Surin's crucially destructive taunting of Hermann for unexpectedly coming face-to-face with the countess at the masked ball—namely that here is his mistress, a deadly catalyst to Hermann's resolution in extracting the secret of the cards from her.

When Hermann announces the first of his bets, the three, the bass trombone ushers in his declaration with the three-cards leitmotif,[16] which the horns, cellos, and double basses then forcefully echo. Prior to this echo, the dotted-rhythm accompaniment arises, evoking those two painful turning points earlier in the opera and pointing the way to Hermann's insane solution for how to circumvent that pain. It is rendered by clarinets and bassoons (on this occasion reinforced by oboes), recalling the instrumentation of its previous deployments, and above that accompaniment, he places his bet. He wins.

His declaration of the second bet, the seven, is preceded by a statement that draws a deeply shocked response from the frequenters of the gambling house: He says he will let his winnings, which are vast, ride. They are increasingly sure he is mad. As he announces that intention, the cards' leitmotif resurges, hushed and surreptitious on the clarinets and bassoons, the clandestine quality underlined by pizzicato cellos and double basses. While the spectators attempt to discourage further bets, and Hermann, regardless, declares the seven, an accompaniment appears in the strings that seems to be a development of the earlier one. This time it is not in dotted rhythm, but like its precursor, it is unremittingly repetitive, as of a driving obsession. However, and most tellingly, it seems to represent a weakening of Hermann's will. That previous rhythm had been strongly demarcated, differentiated internally, as its basic unit (which was constantly repeated) consisted of two notes of which the second lasted for one third of the duration of the first.[17] The strings, conversely, bring in a pattern comprising constant repetitions of a basic unit of three equal elements in terms of duration: two notes of the same denomination as each other, followed by a silence, also of that denomination.[18] That equalization of rhythmic values is, in a sense, not a rhythm at all but merely a pulse—meter instead of rhythm. This may represent a lessening of conscious shaping, a dissipation of the controlling function of Hermann's conscious mind. It further delineates his insanity as something primal emerging into, and overwhelming, conscious reasoning. He wins his second bet, his moment of triumph being preceded by an even louder declaration of the leitmotif of the cards (bassoons plus all of the heaviest-voiced members of the brass section: two tenor trombones, bass trombone, and tuba).

Before his third bet comes an item displaying Hermann's hubris. This too-exuberant and grotesquely self-confident drinking song, delivered with glass in hand, is a mask to the self-destructiveness that is now fatally welling up within him. He declares good and evil to be merely dreams, and, before he has even placed his third bet, announces, "Let the unlucky man weep, cursing his fate!"

It seems that none will now play against this clearly unhinged man. Then Eletsky steps forward. He has accounts to settle with Hermann. As the prince emerges, and just prior to this, as Hermann calls for a playing partner, the leitmotif of the cards returns (a little less forcefully, as there is less need, in view of the inevitable tragedy; cellos and double basses play it, plus a staccato rendition, simultaneously, on two trombones). Preceding Hermann's declaration of his third bet, another repetitive accompaniment occurs, this time a confused mass of different rhythmic values on different instruments, a veritable limbo.[19] Perhaps it stands for Hermann being the victim not only of his weakened and engulfed mind, but of an evil Fate also. His cry "My ace!" is prefaced by a version of the cards' leitmotif incorporating the *diabolus in musica,* the tritone (on a bassoon, the three trombones, tuba, and double basses), unlike all of the other renditions of it in this scene (where a perfect fourth was used instead), but echoing, with deadly fidelity, the clarinet's rendering of it in the opera's opening scene, when Tomsky had first revealed the nickname of the young, gambling-obsessed countess, "The Queen of Spades." Indeed it is right that it be so—Hermann's card is that very one, and not an ace. The countess's ghost appears, while her artificial, whole-tone scale once again hovers in the air (in the dark aspects of clarinets and a bassoon). Hermann stabs himself.

The unaccompanied male chorus's prayer over Hermann's dead body brings a textural and musical simplicity that clears the air of the ingenious accumulation of musical artifice that had conveyed his vain strivings. It establishes, moreover, an associative link to the quotation of Russian Orthodox chant in the scene in Hermann's barracks.[20] It confirms all things as being well in the world, for it extends hope even to his "rebellious and tormented soul."

Of Tchaikovsky's three operas to texts by Pushkin, *Eugene Onegin* had triumphed in the richness of its lyricism, and it had been strongly organized throughout in its articulation of dramatic structure. *Mazeppa* had been less notable as to lyric content per se, but it had delivered intense, if intermittent, moments of the intermeshing of music and drama. Even less noteworthy in purely lyrical terms is *The Queen of Spades*, yet the intertwining of its musical and dramatic framework, despite all the sensational ghost-story aspects of it, but perhaps, indeed, because of their strikingly successful integration with the hero's descent into madness, brought into the international operatic repertoire one of its very greatest dramas.

CHAPTER 10

THE CULMINATING ALLEGORY:
YOLANDE

AFTER TCHAIKOVSKY'S HIGHLY successful collaboration with his
brother on *The Queen of Spades*, Modest again wrote the libretto for the composer's next opera, *Yolande*,[1] basing it on Vladimir Zotov's adaptation of the
Danish author Henrik Hertz's play *Kong Renés Datter* (*King René's Daughter*).
The work was part of a commission from the Imperial Theaters for a one-Act
opera to be performed in a double bill with a two-Act ballet, *The Nutcracker*.
The action of the opera, set in the mountains of southern France in the
fifteenth century, concerns an artificial situation established, with the aim of
protecting the blind Princess Yolande, by her father. The story's single Act
runs as follows:

In a luxuriant garden that is set aside for her as a specially protected haven,
Princess Yolande is in the company of friends and attendants who are for-
bidden by her father, René, king of Provence, from even letting slip any
hint to her that she is blind. Nor does she know her father is king; instead
she has been given to believe he is a wealthy knight. Yet she has become
discontent, despite this idyllic environment. She tells her devoted nurse,
Marthe, "I'm lacking something . . . what?" At this, Marthe weeps, and
Yolande comes and touches her eyes, then asks why she is in tears. Marthe
replies with a question, "Can I be calm when you are crying?" But Marthe
had not touched Yolande's eyes to tell whether or not *she* was crying, and
Yolande had not betrayed her tears through the sound of her voice. So,
asks Yolande, how did Marthe know she was crying? A silence greets the
question and Yolande adds, "No, there's something here which it is impossible for you to tell me!" She asks Marthe if it can really be that eyes are
given only for crying. Nothing seems able to lift Yolande's sadness. She is
presented with flowers (women's chorus), states her thanks, then falls

asleep to a women's chorus of lullaby, and is carried offstage. The empty stage resounds to the call of hunting horns. A messenger, the king's armor-bearer Alméric, arrives; he declares this garden a paradise, and he tells the doorkeeper, Bertrand, that the king is coming with a great Moorish doctor. Bertrand tells Alméric—who was unaware that Yolande was blind and who believed the generally disseminated account that she was in a Spanish convent—the truth: As a baby, she was actually placed here so that her betrothed, Robert, duke of Burgundy, should not learn of her blindness until she had been cured.

King René arrives with the doctor, Ibn Yahya,[2] who exits to examine the sleeping Yolande. In an aria, the king, alone, sings of his anguish at his daughter's condition, of his desperate wish that she be cured, and begs for God to pity him. Ibn Yahya returns and declares that Yolande must be told that she is blind before a cure can be attempted; she must wish her affliction to be overcome, then, indeed, it may be. The king deems her knowing her condition too high a price—what if the treatment fails and she is left knowing she is blind? He dismisses the doctor, but the latter sings his monologue on the duality of existence, on the communion of the physical and the spiritual aspects of being. The doctor tells the king he will wait until evening for his decision, but he will not try to cure Yolande unless his stipulations are met.

After the stage empties, two characters who have lost their way come upon Yolande's garden by chance—one is none other than her betrothed, Duke Robert, and the other his companion, a Burgundian knight, Count Vaudémont. The latter exclaims that this place is a paradise. The duke reads a notice forbidding entry on penalty of death but he is undeterred. Vaudémont has misgivings, but stays because the duke, who also feels this garden is like paradise, wishes to rest after their journey. Ironically, Duke Robert gives as an extra reason for resting here his wish to defer for as long as possible any contact with his fiancée and her father—for he is actually in love with the Countess Mathilde. He bursts into an aria about his feelings for her. Vaudémont, whom love has yet to awaken, finds it when he follows some footprints and reaches a door leading to a terrace; beyond it he sees the sleeping Yolande. He falls instantly in love with her, declaring that she is an angel. The duke, who is quite unmoved at the sight of her, is, unknowingly, setting eyes for the first time in his life on the girl to whom he had been betrothed since childhood. He tries to dissuade his companion from contact with her. Their hubbub awakens her. The duke is unable to hold Vaudémont back from introducing himself. After Yolande leaves to bring wine, the duke departs to fetch soldiers to rescue Vaudémont, whom he considers bewitched. Yolande returns and Vaudémont declares his love to her. When he asks her to pick a rose as a memento of their meeting, and of the hot blush of her cheeks, she picks a white rose instead of the required red one. Once he realizes she is blind, he tells her of her affliction and of the existence of light. He explains to her that it is light that enables him to perceive her beauty.

The king, the doctor, and characters of the royal entourage return. The king is enraged to see the stranger in the garden and asks Vaudémont if he has said anything to Yolande. She herself replies that he has told her about light, and his pity of her for being blind. Although the king sees this as punishment from God, the doctor considers it a blessing in disguise. The king states that Ibn Yahya can cure Yolande and asks her if she wishes to see, but she indicates that it would be hard for her to long for a faculty that she only vaguely comprehends. However, her father hits upon a ploy. He orders that the treatment begin, and then confronts Vaudémont with a question: Did he read the notice that forbids entry, with its threat of mortal punishment? Vaudémont acknowledges he did—upon which the king proclaims that he must die if Yolande's treatment fails. He dismisses his daughter's pleas on Vaudémont's behalf. She declares her willingness to suffer if this will save Vaudémont, and she exits with Ibn Yahya to attempt the cure.

The king now admits to Vaudémont that his threat of death was merely a stratagem to induce Yolande to wish to see. Duke Robert returns accompanied by his soldiers and, upon seeing the king, pays homage. Vaudémont understands for the first time that it is the king with whom he has been dealing. When Duke Robert openly admits to the king that, although he will honor his long-standing pledge to wed Yolande, he loves another, the king respectfully dissolves the agreement and consents to Vaudémont's wish to marry his daughter.

Ibn Yahya returns with Yolande. She can now see. She is fearful, as well as overjoyed, at her new faculty to enjoy God's gift of light. Final chorus to the Almighty.

Yolande, composed in 1891, was first performed at the Mariinsky Theater on 18 December 1892, conducted by Nápravník. Rather than prefacing the opera with an Overture scored for full orchestra, Tchaikovsky opens with one employing only woodwinds and horns. Immediately, the audience is presented with a unique portal through which to pass into the opera itself (in which the full orchestra will, naturally, be used). The most important element missing from the Overture is the orchestral string section. Strings have a degree of warm and flexible tone that makes them the expressive heart of an orchestra. Their omission represents the hero's love that will come to Yolande in the opera, to help her gain sightedness. The use of wind timbre, conversely, stands for Yolande's blindness and related matters, with the woodwind group providing the most clear set of symbolic associations to these features within the opera itself, the horns' connection to the heroine's blindness being mostly confined to the Overture.

We saw in *Mazeppa* and *The Queen of Spades* how Tchaikovsky developed a well-established operatic convention of associating a character's mental disintegration with the utilization of a solo instrument to act as that character's companion and help envelop them in their own, special sound-world. The difference between Hermann in *The Queen of Spades* being paired with a bass clarinet and the heroine of *Yolande* having an association with the orchestra's entire woodwind section, plus horns, is that whereas his affliction is mental, hers is physical and spiritual. Yolande's instruments do not just convey the sense of a special musical realm set aside for her; they also symbolize the literal, physical, and organizational world in which her father has sought to cocoon her. They symbolize the blindness of the world that has been devised for her, as much as her physical blindness, and also the much greater spiritual blindness of her father in preventing her from even knowing she is blind, which ultimately begins to depress her spirit. King René's daughter cannot see his ironically beautiful garden, but others can see that it is, in pure physical terms, like a paradise; Alméric, Vaudémont and Duke Robert all vouch for that.

As Yolande is shielded from the world by attendants whom her father has specially chosen and instructed never to use words connected with seeing and light, her personal environment is a fragile entity whose shattering by the unexpected arrival of the hero, who reveals her blindness to her, sets the drama in motion. Yet this is a singularly undramatic drama. Given a scenario in which a blind heroine can only acquire the sense of sight through a medical treatment in which the prerequisites for success are that she be told of her blindness and that she wishes to vanquish it strongly enough, and in which the strength of necessary will is duly provided by her father's threat that the man she has fallen in love with (and who had innocently ruptured her implausible environment) will otherwise die, no audience is likely to assume anything other than that the heroine will regain her sight and the hero be saved. Following a succession of operas—*The Maid of Orléans, Mazeppa, The Enchantress,* and *The Queen of Spades*—that had all been decidedly operatic, here now was a virtual non-drama with which, as the composer would be dead one year after its premiere, his career as an operatic dramatist happens to end. In a sense, we have come full circle, back to the undramatic nature of Tchaikovsky's first opera, in which the hero's beloved had been taken from him by the eponymous Voevoda, only to be returned to him with the gratuitous arrival on the scene of a new Voevoda replacing the villainous one. However, what is really significant about *Yolande* is not its dramatic status but its richly allegorical character.

Fundamental to the allegory is the recurrent sounding of fanfares in the opera, the most significant being the first set of these, which occur in a brief orchestral interlude and symbolically herald the arrival of a royal messenger, Alméric, with news that the king will arrive with a great Moorish doctor.

They sound just after Yolande, sensing for the first time that something is amiss in her world and that other people seem to have a degree of perception that she lacks, has been lulled to sleep by her companions. Moreover, the fanfares, played by horns, are interspersed with reminiscences, delicately rendered by oboes, then flutes, of that preceding women's lullaby-chorus. These musical echoes have a touchingly fragrant charm because this enchantingly implausible, sleepy world surrounding Yolande will soon be plunged into the outside world's realities, as depicted by the fanfaring horns' warning signals. The interlude ends with yet another fanfare, but on this occasion played by trumpets and occurring, as it were, in real time, betokening Alméric's actual, impending entry onstage (whereas the interaction of instruments in the preceding music gives the effect of a ruminative and philosophical discussion).

When King René appears, announced by another fanfare, with the physician Ibn Yahya, the latter examines the sleeping Yolande and declares that she might be cured, but only upon the condition that her father finds objectionable: that she be told of her infirmity. Because the doctor cannot meet the king's demand for an assurance that if his daughter is so informed, the treatment will definitely succeed, there is an impasse. The second crack then appears in the ornamental world surrounding Yolande, the first having been her own perception, at the start of the opera, that something was unaccounted for in her life. Ibn Yahya tells the king of the lack of self-sufficiency of the mortal body, that the body is linked with the spirit, and René begins to wonder if keeping an awareness of his daughter's condition from her has actually impeded her chances of recovery.

Circumstances now break the impasse. Interestingly, although the arrival of the king, and the messenger, had been signaled by offstage fanfares, none now heralds the entry of the character, Count Vaudémont, who provides the third—and decisive—crack in Yolande's fragile sphere. Nothing will be the same again in René and Yolande's world after Vaudémont and his friend Duke Robert have chanced upon this garden, merely to rest from their journey. The purity of this as yet unviolated, and, in itself, blind, realm is emphasized by a flowing stream of arpeggios on piccolo, flutes, clarinets, and bassoons as the two strangers enter, the woodwind associations of René's deceptive environment for his daughter floridly reiterated. Vaudémont sings, "With my own eyes do I see paradise amid wild crags!"

It is remarkably ironic that Robert has turned up, without knowing it, in Yolande's domain, because his childhood betrothal to her is an obstacle to his present desires. Not only has he never actually seen her, he wishes, more to the point, never to see her, as he has since found his true love, Mathilde. The music in which he eulogizes Mathilde is decidedly meager in inspiration, however, and constitutes an indubitable flaw. The full, happy resolution of the plot involves Robert's eventual relinquishing of marital claims to Yolande (and the king's corresponding releasing of him from the agreement) so that Vaudémont may become her spouse. If his love of his own inamorata had been more strongly portrayed in the music, it might have suggested the boundless joys of love expressed in the actual words that he sings, and, more important, it could have added substance thereby to the poignant, allegorical irony of his wishing, in effect, that Yolande, as threat to the fulfillment of that love, become invisible to the world. He declares a wish that she "vanish without trace." That is the counterpart of her father's unwitting cruelty in making her spiritually invisible to herself (by denying her the due knowledge of her affliction).

Conversely, Tchaikovsky achieved, in the melody that accompanies Vaudémont's first sight of Yolande, a genuinely intense expression of love, such that one could indeed believe that the heroine might regain her sight through faith in its power. Its shape is strongly profiled, its exuberant leaps recalling Abraham's analogy that Tchaikovsky's most typical melodies are like characterful handwriting.[3] The use of orchestration here is also masterly. The door of the terrace through which Vaudémont will see the sleeping Yolande is not locked, and it opens at his merest touch. As he opens it, the woodwind flutterings of Yolande's world recur, on flutes, oboe, and clarinets, bolstered by the richness of harp arpeggios. But, when he catches sight of her, there is a symbolic switch to string timbre, for the orchestral string section presents the love-music, the melody itself in the vibrant warmth of the cellos, while the remaining strings, with support from timpani, deliver the accompaniment. Two bassoons play in unison with the cellos, adding to the richness of sound, but masked by the cellos' greater loudness. This combination of stringed and woodwind instruments may nevertheless have been intended symbolically, portending a joining, respectively, of Vaudémont's healing love and Yolande herself, in her unhealed state (although such a doubling, to enhance the characterfulness of the sound, is a common feature of nineteenth-century orchestration). There can hardly be any doubt, however, about the allegorical significance of the presentation of the melody that accompanies Yolande's first words when, at the end of the opera, Ibn Yahya's medical treatment of her—combined with her need to save her beloved's life—succeeds. Now able to see, Yolande sings, "Where am I? Where are you taking me, doctor?" while in the background a solo flute gently plays a melody derived from the opening six tones of the theme that had depicted Vaudémont's instantaneous feeling of love upon first beholding the heroine. The flute, representing the woodwind-associated world of the blindness that had afflicted Yolande, makes obeisance, as it were, to the great love-melody that had represented the emotional force that has now enabled her to be relieved of it. It is a moment of great poetic beauty, all the more moving for its subtlety and delicacy. There is no question of this flute variant of Vaudémont's love-melody in any way challenging the lyrical power of the original.

There is no need. Love has done its job. Only for something that has yet to be achieved would greater lyricism be necessary.

Yolande may be a surprising conclusion to Tchaikovsky's succession of operas. Its status as a one-Act drama of course itself puts it in a unique category within that context. But it is not *lightweight*; it can and does readily occupy an evening's entertainment in its own right, without the intended support of its ballet-partner in the double bill. In Russia *Yolande* holds a contemporary place as a repertory item on the opera stage, and in Britain it has also gained some currency, complementing that of *Eugene Onegin* and *The Queen of Spades.* The gentler, more intimate aspects of *Onegin,* indeed, find expression again in *Yolande.* In other respects too *Yolande* may be compared with its predecessors. For example, the descending whole-tone scale, à la Glinka, appears when the heroine temporarily experiences fear through the new sensation of being able to see. That very human context develops the scale's usage in the supernatural setting of the appearance of the countess's ghost in *The Queen of Spades* (evoking Hermann's fear), and of Chub and Panas's unhappy excursion in the Devil's snowstorm in *Vakula the Smith.* The neo-classical *Minuet* in *Vakula* and the substantial interlude in related style in *The Queen of Spades* are echoed at the start of *Yolande* in music for a small ensemble of strings and harp that serenades the princess. The use of an imitation of late eighteenth-century style[4] is, of course, historically misplaced for *Yolande's* fifteenth-century setting, but the quiet dignity of this opening scene well establishes the overall mood of the opera. The story's location did, however, lead Tchaikovsky to avoid any real suggestion of Russian style, and, perhaps even more so than with *The Maid of Orléans,* the prevailing musical characteristics of *Yolande* are French (entirely excluding the rhetorical, grand-opera features of that earlier work, but strongly reflecting its more sweetly lyrical moments).

As for trends in Tchaikovsky's late operas, *Yolande* demonstrates, like *The Queen of Spades,* increasing signs of interest in Wagnerian methods. In many passages in these two scores, the singers' lines are rendered in recitative-like declamation while the orchestra actually holds the main musical weight and structure. For example, in *Yolande,* Vaudémont does not actually sing the great melody expressing his enchantment upon catching sight of the heroine. While the cellos and bassoons play it, he engages in short snatches of sung dialogue with Robert, about the intensity of his feelings. Similarly, the transformation of Vaudémont's passionate love-theme as an ethereal flute melody of similar shape while the love-transformed heroine likewise sings recitative in the background is a feature of decidedly Wagnerian configuration. Even so, Tchaikovsky was merely expanding the range of his available techniques as an opera composer, and he would have had a very long way to go before the assimilation of Wagner's procedures had fundamentally changed his approach. That remained flexible and deeply inventive, as the strikingly original Overture to *Yolande* reveals. Tchaikovsky was as likely to do something entirely new as he was to quote a well-worn element of musical vocabulary drawn from Glinka or, indeed, to make a surprising rapprochement to the compositional techniques of Wagner, which he had condemned over the years in such a determined manner.

Tchaikovsky's embracing experience of life made him avoid commitment to rigidly defined compositional systems. That, no doubt, was his principal ally in realizing—in dramatic and musical terms—the many characters and situations that he had brought so convincingly to life in that great range of stage works—and range of great stage works—that constitute his operas.

CHRONOLOGY OF TCHAIKOVSKY'S LIFE AND MAJOR COMPOSITIONS

1840   Birth of Pëtr Il'ich Tchaikovsky, 7 May, in Votkinsk, in the Viatka region of Russia. He is the second child of his father Ilia's second marriage, to Alexandra Assier; has an elder brother, Nikolai (and a half-sister, Zinaida, from the earlier marriage). Four siblings would follow: sister Alexandra, brother Ippolit, and twin brothers Anatoly and Modest.

1844   Makes first known attempt at composition, aged four, working out by ear, allegedly with his sister Alexandra (then aged not quite two), a song called "Our Mama in Petersburg" in honor of their mother, who was absent on a visit to the capital city. He begins education with the family's French governess, Mlle. Fanny Dürbach.

1845   Is taught piano at elementary level by a freed serf, Maria Palchikova.

1850   Enters preparatory class at the School of Jurisprudence, St. Petersburg.

1854   Mother dies of cholera. He subsequently composes the first piece he is known to have committed to paper (as distinct from the many improvisations he had wrought at the piano since childhood), the *Anastasie Valse* for piano, dedicated to his former governess (Mlle. Dürbach's successor) Anastasia Petrova, who had tutored him for entry into the School of Jurisprudence.

1855   Studies piano with Rudolf Kündinger.

1856   Becomes friends with a singing teacher, Luigi Piccioli, who encourages in him a deep interest in nineteenth-century Italian opera.

1859   Graduates from the School of Jurisprudence and begins work as a clerk at the Ministry of Justice.

1861   Studies musical theory and harmony with Nikolai Zaremba, a strict pedagogue, in classes at the Russian Musical Society (the institution which formed the basis of the St. Petersburg Conservatoire, founded in the following year). Zaremba's insistence on methodical procedures is to be an invaluable counterbalance to the young Tchaikovsky's often undisciplined creativity.

1862   Enrolls at the St. Petersburg Conservatoire.

1863   Makes definitive break from career in the civil service by resigning from the Ministry of Justice.

1864   Composes his first great orchestral work, the overture *The Storm* (based on Ostrovsky's play of that title), as a student exercise. It outrages his tutor, the Conservatoire's director, Anton Rubinstein, by its advanced orchestration and lack of structural cohesion according, at any rate, to his conservative views on those matters. It demonstrates its composer's sense of musical independence, which would be a lifelong characteristic.

1866   Graduates from the St. Petersburg Conservatoire. Begins work as professor of musical theory at the Moscow Conservatoire, founded by Anton Rubinstein's brother Nikolai in the wake of the success of the St. Petersburg prototype. Although a reluctant teacher, Tchaikovsky was thus in the vanguard of professional, institutional musical education in Russia, which the Rubinstein brothers initiated. Indeed, he would presently write two pedagogical texts, *A Guide to the Practical Study of Harmony* (Moscow, 1872) and *A Short Manual of Harmony, Adapted to the Study of Religious Music in Russia* (Moscow, 1875). The latter, which was written in response to a request from the Russian Synod, is a work that forms a natural, didactic counterpart to his output of liturgical music.

        Composes the First Symphony in G minor, overworking in the process and subjecting himself to nervous exhaustion, with sleep-deprivation inducing hallucinations.

1867   Begins writing his first opera, *The Voevoda*.

1868   Carries out his first work as a music critic, writing for *The Contemporary Chronicle*. Completes *The Voevoda*. Considers marriage to the Belgian soprano Désirée Artôt. Composes the symphonic poem *Fatum* ("Fate").

1869   News that Artôt, in the end, married another singer, the Spanish baritone Mariano Padilla y Ramos, temporarily shocks Tchaikovsky, but has no deeper effect. Premiere of *The Voevoda*. Composes the opera *Undine*. Composes the fantasy-overture *Romeo and Juliet* (based on Shakespeare's play) at the suggestion, and even under the guidance, of the idiosyncratic and dictatorial composer Mily Balakirev (1837–1910), leader of the St. Petersburg-based group of avowedly nationalist composers dubbed the "Mighty Handful" or (outside of Russia itself) "The Five" the remaining members being Nikolai Rimsky-Korsakov (1844–1908), César Cui (1835–1918), Modest Musorgsky (1839–81), and Alexander Borodin (1833–87). Tchaikovsky had an ambivalent respect for the group (to which he never belonged), most strongly admiring Balakirev's and Rimsky-Korsakov's creative gifts, despising Cui for reviewing his work in the most vituperative and stilted terms (Cui's notices of his friends' work was, however, no less barbed), loathing Musorgsky's music for what he felt was its untutored barbarity, and maintaining a relative indifference to Borodin's compositions. Tchaikovsky's early works show him at his closest to the nationalist aspirations of the Mighty Handful (*The Voevoda* being a good illustration, displaying strong Russian folk-influence). His style will become increasingly cosmopolitan, however, from around 1876 onwards.

1870   Begins writing the opera *The Oprichnik*. The Imperial Theaters' directorate in St. Petersburg rejects *Undine*, which is to be the only one of Tchaikovsky's operas never to reach the stage. Revises *Romeo and Juliet*, in accordance with Balakirev's suggestions.

1871   Composes the First String Quartet in D major.

1872   Completes *The Oprichnik*. Composes the Second Symphony in C minor.

1873   Like Balakirev before him, Vladimir Stasov, propagandist for the Mighty Handful, extends his influence beyond the group and suggests that Tchaikovsky write an orchestral evocation of Shakespeare's *The Tempest*; the resulting symphonic fantasia of that title is, indeed, based on a program devised by Stasov.

1874   Composes the Second String Quartet in F major. Premiere of *The Oprichnik*. Composes the opera *Vakula the Smith*. Begins writing the First Piano Concerto in B flat minor.

1875   Completes the First Piano Concerto. Composes the Third Symphony in D major. Begins writing his first ballet, *Swan Lake* (based on a fairytale source, possibly of German origin), in which he places ballet music on a historically new, symphonic footing.

1876   Attends Bizet's opera *Carmen* in Paris, which captivates him. Composes the Third String Quartet in E flat minor. Completes *Swan Lake*. Deeply loathes Wagner's tetralogy of operas *Der Ring des Nibelungen* (*The Nibelung's Ring*), the first complete performance of which, at Bayreuth, he reviews for *The Russian Register*. Composes the symphonic fantasia *Francesca da Rimini* (based on Dante's *Inferno*), the first work to show all the characteristics of his middle period, namely heightened emotionalism, reduced use of Russian folk style, and increased cosmopolitanism. Premiere of *Vakula the Smith*. Composes the *Variations on a Rococo Theme* for cello and orchestra. Begins correspondence with a wealthy widow, Nadezhda von Meck, who had commissioned him (through an intermediary) to arrange some of his music for violin and piano. This purely epistolary relationship would continue for the next fourteen years (she and he never met) in a vast outpouring of letters. She would provide him with emotional and financial support in an undeniably intense relationship that, however, came to a devastatingly sudden end, for reasons that are still unclear.

1877   Premiere of *Swan Lake*. Begins writing the Fourth Symphony in F minor in which, for the first time, his work as a symphonist sufficiently intensifies in architectural strength and inspiration for him to be seen as cutting a dynamic, new post-Beethovenian path, as distinctive as the symphonic developments being explored by his Austrian contemporary Bruckner (1824–96) and portending the work of Rakhmaninov (1873–1943), Prokofiev (1891–1953), and Shostakovich (1906–1975) by providing alternative paradigms to the usual teutonic ones. Tchaikovsky may thus be viewed as being as much the father of the Russian symphony as Haydn (1732–1809) was of the symphony itself; he brought Russian symphonism into the cosmopolitan mainstream. Begins writing the opera *Eugene Onegin*. Marriage to Antonina Miliukova, purely with intention of discouraging gossip about his homosexuality. His marriage collapses, he has a nervous breakdown, and he leaves for a recuperative stay in Switzerland and other European locations. Mrs. von Meck begins paying him what would turn out to be a substantial and regular subsidy, which would presently enable him to free himself of the constraints of earning a daily living, and devote himself entirely to composition.

1878   Completes the Fourth Symphony and *Eugene Onegin*. Composes the Violin Concerto in D major. Composes the Liturgy of St. John Chrysostom. Begins writing the First Orchestral Suite in D minor. Resigns from the Moscow Conservatoire and commences a wandering existence that would continue for the next seven years, passing in and out of Europe and Russia, with no real home of his own but with a surrogate home at the estate of his sister Alexandra at Kamenka in the Ukraine. Begins writing the opera *The Maid of Orléans*.

1879   Premiere of *Eugene Onegin*. Completes *The Maid of Orléans*. Begins writing the Second Piano Concerto in G major.

1880   Father dies. Completes the Second Piano Concerto. Revises *Romeo and Juliet* for the second time. This definitive version (different in many ways from the original) is among the most intense expressions of love in nineteenth-century music. Composes the Serenade in C major for Strings. Composes the festival overture, *1812* (commemorating Napoleon's defeat by Russian forces in that year).

1881   Premiere of *The Maid of Orléans*. Begins writing the Vesper Service. Begins writing the opera *Mazeppa*. Begins writing the Piano Trio in A minor, in memory of Nikolai Rubinstein, who died in this year.

1882   Completes the Piano Trio and the Vesper Service.

1883   Completes *Mazeppa*. Composes the Second Orchestral Suite in C major.

1884   Premiere of *Mazeppa*. Composes the Third Orchestral Suite in G major, the last in the series of original compositions that comprise the suites (a Fourth Orchestral Suite in G major, entitled *Mozartiana*, would follow in 1887, but this is a set of arrangements of pieces by Mozart, rather than an original work). The suites were strangely suited to the travelling existence that was Tchaikovsky's lot in the aftermath of the marriage fiasco. They are highly uneven but intermittently brilliant, and are exploratory in style and construction, sometimes strikingly so (for example, the experimental nature of the First Orchestral Suite's *Gavotte* anticipates Prokofiev's side-stepping shifts of key). They are rarely encountered in the concert hall, with the exception of the Third Orchestral Suite's finale, which is sometimes performed as a separate item, although the remaining movements of that work are no less richly inventive and contain some of the most unduly neglected orchestral music of the Romantic period. Composes the Concert Fantasia for piano and orchestra.

1885   Rents a home at Maidanovo, outside Moscow, and thus brings the rootless life he had pursued since 1878 to a close. Revises *Vakula the Smith* under the new title *Cherevichki*. Composes the *Manfred* Symphony (based on Byron's poem) at Balakirev's suggestion, to a program derived (although Balakirev did not name the adapter) by Stasov from the poem.

Although inconsistent, *Manfred* arguably contains some of the greatest music Tchaikovsky had written since the Fourth Symphony. It also marks the most important stylistic shift in his work since 1876, establishing his third, and final, period. The notable new characteristics are a heightened use of dissonance, and darker woodwind scoring than previously (which exploits low registers, and unison combinations in low and medium compasses). Begins writing the opera *The Enchantress.*

1887   Premiere of *Cherevichki.* Completes *The Enchantress,* and, as with *Cherevichki,* conducts the premiere himself. Embarks on concert tours of the West in his increasingly prestigious new role of conductor (the last major professional development to occur in his life, discounting extremely sporadic appearances in this role in earlier years).

1888   Composes the Fifth Symphony in E minor and the fantasy-overture *Hamlet* (based on Shakespeare's play). Begins writing the ballet *The Sleeping Beauty* (based on Perrault's *La belle au bois dormant).*

1889   Completes *The Sleeping Beauty.*

1890   Premiere of *The Sleeping Beauty.* Composes the opera *The Queen of Spades,* and the String Sextet in D minor, *Souvenir de Florence* (whose opening had been sketched in 1887). Begins writing the symphonic ballad *The Voevoda* (based on Pushkin's free translation of a poem by the Polish poet Mickiewicz) which, despite the title, has no connection with his first opera. During work on it, he receives word from Mrs. von Meck of her decision to break off their relationship. She seems to claim her wealth had collapsed (which in fact was not so) and that his allowance from her would have to end. His remaining years are embittered by the thought that she had believed the only meaningful link between them was financial. Premiere of *The Queen of Spades.*

1891   Begins writing the ballet *The Nutcracker* (based on Dumas *père's* version of E. T. A. Hoffmann's *Nussknacker und Mausekönig*) and composes the opera *Yolande,* commissioned to be performed together as a double bill. Completes *The Voevoda* before finishing *Yolande.*

1892   Completes *The Nutcracker.* Premiere of *Yolande* and *The Nutcracker.*

1893   Composes the Sixth Symphony in B minor (the *Pathétique),* and adapts the opening movement of an abortive symphony in E flat major, upon which he had worked the previous year, to be his single-movement Third Piano Concerto in E flat major. Dies of cholera, in St. Petersburg, on 6 November.

LIST OF TCHAIKOVSKY'S OPERAS WITH GENERAL DATA

Title	Authorship of Libretto	Dates of Composition
The Voevoda	Ostrovsky and the composer, after Ostrovsky's *The Voevoda,* or *A Dream on the Volga*	1867–68
Undine	V. Sollogub, after Zhukovsky's trans. of F. H. K. de la Motte Fouqué	1869
The Oprichnik	The composer, after Ivan Lazhechnikov's *The Oprichniks*	1870–72
Vakula the Smith, rev. and retitled *Cherevichki*	*Vakula the Smith:* I. Polonsky, after Gogol's *Christmas Eve.* *Cherevichki:* The revision was carried out by the composer	*Vakula the Smith:* 1874 *Cherevichki:* 1885
Eugene Onegin	The composer and Konstantin Shilovsky, after Pushkin	1877–78
The Maid of Orléans	The composer, after Zhukovsky's trans. of Schiller; also these important sources: the opera *Jeanne d'Arc,* by A. Mermet, and the play of the same title by J. Barbier	1878–79; rev. 1882
Mazeppa	V. Burenin, after Pushkin's *Poltava,* and rev. by the composer	1881–83
The Enchantress	Ippolit Shpazhinsky, rev. by the composer	1885–87
The Queen of Spades	Modest Tchaikovsky (the composer's brother), after Pushkin, and rev. by the composer; various other sources also adapted	1890
Yolande	Modest Tchaikovsky, after V. Zotov's adaptation of Henrik Hertz's *Kong Renés Datter* (*King René's Daughter*)	1891

Date and Place of Premiere	Conductor of Premiere	Additional Information
11 February 1869, Bolshoi Theater, Moscow	Eduard Merten	Although the composer eventually destroyed the score of the opera, it was reconstructed by Soviet scholars using the Bolshoi Theater's archival performing parts and other material.
Never staged		The composer destroyed the score of the opera in 1875. As no production of the opera had occurred, no performing parts were prepared from which a reconstruction might be attempted.
24 April 1874, Mariinsky Theater, St. Petersburg	Eduard Nápravník	The composer conceived an aversion to the opera and expressed a wish to revise it (although he never did so).
Vakula the Smith: 6 December 1876, Mariinsky Theater *Cherevichki:* 31 January 1887, Bolshoi Theater	*Vakula the Smith:* Nápravník. *Cherevichki:* the composer.	The composer's only genuine comic opera (there are merely traces of comedy in *The Voevoda*).
29 March 1879, Maly Theater, Moscow	Nikolai Rubinstein	Écossaise was added to Act 3 scene 1 in 1885.
25 February 1881, Mariinsky Theater	Nápravník	This was the first of the composer's operas to be performed outside Russia (Prague, 28 July 1882, in Czech trans.).
15 February 1884, Bolshoi Theater	Ippolit Altani	Three days after the Moscow premiere, the opera was performed at the Mariinsky Theater, a sign of the composer's growing fame.
1 November 1887, Mariinsky Theater	The composer	The composer held this to be the greatest opera that he had yet written (letter to Shpazhinsky, early May 1888).
19 December 1890, Mariinsky Theater	Nápravník	This opera is a musical counterpart to Russia's literary "Silver Age" (the period from the 1890s to the Russian Civil War).
18 December 1892, Mariinsky Theater	Nápravník	This is the composer's only opera in a single Act (it was composed as a double bill with the two-Act ballet *The Nutcracker*).

NOTES

Preface

1. Roland John Wiley, *Tchaikovsky's Ballets* (Oxford, 1985), 276.
2. David Brown, *Tchaikovsky: A Biographical and Critical Study*, vol. 2, *The Crisis Years (1874–1878)* (London, 1982), 218.
3. The year given for an event will, of course, be affected if the discrepancy between the two dating systems dictates it (e.g., the composer Mily Balakirev was born on 2 January 1837 "New-Style," but that date would be stated as 21 December 1836 if the "Old-Style" calendar is used).

Chapter 1

1. Tchaikovsky destroyed the score of *Undine* in 1875. For reasons proposed by Gerald Abraham (see the chapter entitled "Tchaïkovsky's Operas" in *Slavonic and Romantic Music* (London, 1968), 125–26) it seems possible that the composer did not destroy the score of *The Voevoda* until many years had elapsed.
2. The first staged production of *The Maid of Orléans* in Great Britain was given by soloists and chorus of the Bolshoi Opera, conducted by Alexander Lazarev, on 10 August 1990 at the Scottish Exhibition and Conference Centre, Glasgow.
3. The present author's earlier assessment of this opera (see Henry Zajaczkowski, *Tchaikovsky's Musical Style* (Ann Arbor/London, 1987), 144) was largely mistaken.
4. As translated by M.D. Calvocoressi in his chapter on Liadov in Calvocoressi and Gerald Abraham, *Masters of Russian Music* (London, 1936), 427.
5. Tchaikovsky's late period began in 1885 with the *Manfred* Symphony. That work marks a significant darkening in his musical language, both in terms of harmony—for instance, an increased use of successive seventh chords, whose unresolved dissonance often produces an effect of unrelieved yearning (and cf. the observations concerning Manfredian harmony in *The Enchantress*, in chapter 8)—and orchestration, for example in a textural thickening of the woodwind parts, through instruments of different denomination (such as oboe and clarinet) being put in unison, in their low and medium registers (cf. too the assessment of comparable features in *The Queen of Spades*, in chapter 9).

6. Quoted by Donald C. Seibert in "The Dramaturgy of Tchaikovsky's *Mazeppa*: An Interview with Mark Elder," *Music Review* 49 (1988): 275.

7. See Gerald Seaman's article "The Rise of Russian Opera" in *The New Oxford History of Music*, vol. 7, ed. Egon Wellesz and Frederick Sternfeld, *The Age of Enlightenment* (London/New York/ Toronto, 2nd impression 1974), 273.

8. Richard Taruskin gives a detailed and cogent account of the issues Russian composers faced in addressing Glinka's influence in the first chapter, entitled "Glinka's Ambiguous Legacy and the Birth Pangs of Russian Opera," of *Opera and Drama in Russia As Preached and Practiced in the 1860s* (Ann Arbor, 1981).

9. The melody of this aria well conveys the contours and spirit of Russian folk song, but was nevertheless, it seems, Glinka's own.

10. As translated by Taruskin, *Opera and Drama*, 2.

11. David Brown, *Mikhail Glinka: A Biographical and Critical Study* (London, 1974), 228.

12. A scale in which each successive pitch is separated by a whole tone. With its absolutely uniform landscape, with no distinguishing features, the whole-tone scale can give the ear a sense of feeling lost.

13. In *Swan Lake*, the B minor *scène* at the start of Act 2 (famous for its oboe melody) has a passing whole-tone scale, in the bass, symbolizing the evil magic of the heroine's stepmother. See Brown, *Tchaikovsky*, vol. 2, 84, and musical example 118. In the *Manfred* Symphony's finale, the brief use of the whole-tone scale at one point, also in the bass line, reinforces the depiction of the supernatural, as this movement represents a bacchanal in the infernal palace of Arimanes, according to the work's program. See Zajaczkowski, *Tchaikovsky's Musical Style*, 70, and musical example 26.

Chapter 2

1. References to the text and music of *The Voevoda* are to the reconstruction of the opera by a team of scholars headed by P. A. Lamm, published as vols. 1a, 1b, 1c, and 1 suppl. of P. Chaikovskii, *Polnoe sobranie sochinenii* (Complete Collected Works) (Moscow, 1953).

2. In *A Life for the Tsar*, Glinka used a Russian folk song that he himself had transcribed from the singing of a Luga coachman, also the famous "Down by Mother Volga," and possibly a third folk song, too, said by Daria Leonova to have been heard by the composer as it was being sung by another coachman as he was passing by Smolensk. See Brown, *Glinka*, 111–12 and note 1 on the latter page.

3. Brown points out (*ibid.*, 48) that the melody of this chorus seems to be of authentic Persian origin and that Glinka acquired it through the singing of a secretary at the Persian embassy.

4. The first of these folk songs was given to Tchaikovsky, in actual musical notation, by Ostrovsky himself. The second was transcribed by Tchaikovsky from a peasant woman's singing, in Kuntsevo, near Moscow. All three appear, in the same order as that in which they occur in the opera, as items 23–25 in Tchaikovsky's collection, arranged for piano duet, of *50 Russian Folksongs* (1868–69).

5. The *Entr'acte and Dance of the Serving-Maids* is adapted from the *Characteristic Dances* for orchestra (1865).

6. The song never settles into any clear metrical pattern, moving with ease between septuple, quintuple, triple, and sextuple meters.

7. As translated by Abraham, *Slavonic and Romantic Music*, 117.

8. Brown, *Tchaikovsky*, vol. 1, *The Early Years (1840–1874)* (London, 1978), 149.

9. *Ibid.*, 148.

10. It is perhaps particularly significant, in this regard, that Tchaikovsky built the development sections in his symphonic movements less from an organic and interwoven handling of short musical fragments (the typical Germanic method) than by juxtaposing blocks of music several measures or more in length, thereby interrupting and suppressing the sense of flow until the tension mounts to find release in a final climax of immense force. That climax paradoxically provides both severance—as the culminating point of the development section—and an ineluctable confirmation of that whole section's architectural strength, whose underlying propulsive force was so great that suppression was necessary to guide and shape it. That is an achievement of such artistic integrity that it transcends the usual charge made against Tchaikovsky's symphonic developmental technique: that it is unsubtle. (Cf. the present writer's account of "suppressive-propulsive" methods in Tchaikovsky's procedures for joining the sections within a work, his symphonic development sections, and his music in general, in the first two chapters and elsewhere in *Tchaikovsky's Musical Style*; cf. also, in the present text, the appraisal of similar methods in *The Oprichnik*, in chapter 3 and note 11; *Eugene Onegin*, in chapter 5 and notes 15 and 20; *Mazeppa*, in chapter 7 and note 3; *The Enchantress*, in chapter 8 and note 2; and *The Queen of Spades*, in chapter 9 and note 10.)

A vitally important factor in Wagner's building of large-scale operatic structures, on the other hand, is his adaptation of the discussional subtleties of the traditional Germanic symphonic development section.

11. Abraham, *Slavonic and Romantic Music*, 117.

12. *Ibid.*, 130.

13. *Ibid.*, 131.

Chapter 3

1. However, there was a well received, staged revival at the Bolshoi Theater on 6 March 1999, conducted by Mark Ermler, demonstrating that *The Oprichnik* merits regeneration. I am grateful to Alexander Poznansky for information (in a personal communication) about this performance.

2. See Philip Taylor, *The Oprichnik, an Opera in 4 Acts, Libretto and Music by Pyotr Il'ich Tchaikovsky: Translation and Notes* (London and Wellingborough, 1980), 14.

3. As translated by Taylor, *ibid.*, 19.

4. In mitigation, however, it should be said that Tchaikovsky faced objections from the censor as to portraying Ivan the Terrible onstage, so that the composer made Viazminsky function as mouthpiece for the Tsar, who never, indeed, appears in the opera.

5. Abraham, *Slavonic and Romantic Music*, 130. For a list of large blocks of material transferred from *The Voevoda* to *The Oprichnik* and of smaller-scale borrowings, see Taylor, *The Oprichnik*, 27 (also 21).

6. As translated by Taylor, *ibid.*, 19.

7. As translated by Taylor, *ibid.*, 47.

8. Richard Taruskin, "'The Present in the Past': Russian Opera and Russian Historiography, ca. 1870," in *Russian and Soviet Music: Essays for Boris Schwarz*, ed. Malcolm Hamrick Brown (Ann Arbor, 1984), 86.

9. Taruskin reveals how effective Tchaikovsky's modification of Lazhechnikov's text was, the words of the chorus of townsfolk being adapted from the speeches of the noblemen Fëdorov and Viskovatov in Act 3 scene 3 of the original play, those of Morozova's arioso from her text in Act 2 scene 6, and those of the chorus of boys who taunt Morozova from their text in Act 3 scene 1. He furthermore suggests that the composer might have had the basic idea of Natalia running away from home and asking Morozova to protect her, an incident not in Lazhechnikov, from her abduction by Andrei in Act 4 scene 1 of the play. See *ibid.*, 87–88.

10. *Ibid.*, 90.

11. This is another permutation, and indeed a particularly subtle one, of Tchaikovsky's "suppressive-propulsive" compositional technique, described in note 10 to chapter 2. Usually there is a far clearer sense of release when the propulsive moment comes than the feeling of suspense displayed here. The rich psychological ambiguities of the situation are well conveyed by the composer (cf. also note 10 to chapter 9). As concerns the psychological aspects in general of Tchaikovsky's suppressive-propulsive methods, see the present author's *Tchaikovsky's Musical Style*, 137–38, and "On Čajkovskij's Psychopathology and Its Relationship with His Creativity," *Čajkovskij-Studien* [*Tchaikovsky Studies*], 1 (1995; the published form of papers read at the International Tchaikovsky Symposium, Tübingen, 1993): 307–28.

Chapter 4

1. Galina von Meck, trans., *"To My Best Friend": Correspondence between Tchaikovsky and Nadezhda von Meck, 1876–1878*, ed. Edward Garden and Nigel Gotteri (Oxford, 1993), 363–64, Tchaikovsky's letter of 11 Nov. 1878.

2. No full score of *Vakula the Smith* has been published, although extracts from it appear in a set of appendices to P. Chaikovskii, *Polnoe sobranie sochinenii* [henceforth P.S.S.], vol. 35 (Moscow, 1956), 333–420. The main part of that volume is a complete vocal score of the opera. For the full-score version of the snowstorm music, see m.387 *et seq.* (from the marking: *L'istesso Tempo*), 350 onwards (and for the corresponding location in the vocal score: *ibid.*, 70 onwards). For the recast snowstorm music in the full score of *Cherevichki*, see m.128 *et seq.* (from the marking: *Allegro moderato*) in P.S.S., vol. 7(a) (Moscow/Leningrad, 1951), 121 onwards (and for the corresponding location in the vocal score: P.S.S., vol. 39 (Moscow/Leningrad, 1951), 54 onwards). See also note 13, following.

3. The motif E-D sharp-E, comprising three eighth-notes and repeated throughout mm.191–92 of item 10 of the vocal score of *Vakula the Smith*, is transformed into sixteenth-notes in m.193, and then diminished still further into triplet sixteenth-notes in m.194. From that point, and into the subsequent measures, a great proliferation of other semitonal motifs (e.g., B-A sharp-B), also cast as triplet sixteenth-notes, suddenly occurs, as the chorus and Oksana engage in the frantic fun of their snowball fight. See P.S.S., vol. 35, 174 *et seq.*, and the corresponding full-score fragment (which, however, is only printed from m.193 onwards), *ibid.*, 403 *et seq.* For the version of the snowball fight in *Cherevichki*, see m.142 *et seq.* of item 14 (P.S.S., vol. 7 (a)), 369 onwards.

4. As translated by Philip Taylor in *Gogolian Interludes: Gogol's Story 'Christmas Eve' as the Subject of the Operas by Tchaikovsky and Rimsky-Korsakov* (London and Wellingborough, 1984), 244.

5. See m.7 in item 8 of *Vakula the Smith* (P.S.S., vol. 35), 147.

6. The closing scene of *Vakula the Smith* (Act 3 scene 4) was officially redesignated as the closing Act (i.e., Act 4) of *Cherevichki*, as part of the process of revision (although at the premiere of *Vakula* it had, in fact, been rendered as a separate Act). The chromatic lament occurs to the following text, which is sung in duet:

Oksana: "Ah, the pain, the pain, there is no joy in my allotted joy. . . ."

Solokha: "Oh, sun of my life! Oh, where have you set!"

See mm.80–83 in item 19 of *Vakula the Smith* (P.S.S., vol. 35), 301; and, the same measure references in item 24 of *Cherevichki* (P.S.S., vol. 39), 338.

7. See m.134 *et seq.* in item 20 of *Vakula the Smith* (P.S.S., vol. 35), 315; and, m.186 *et seq.* in item 25 of *Cherevichki* (P.S.S., vol. 39), 355.

8. See mm.58–59 and m.64 in item 15 of *Vakula the Smith* (P.S.S., vol. 35), 260; and the same measure references in item 21 of *Cherevichki* (P.S.S., vol. 39), 306.

9. Rimsky-Korsakov's earlier opera, *The Snow Maiden* (first version 1880–81) also made use of a text originally employed by the elder composer, for the play by Ostrovsky upon which it is based had been provided with incidental music by Tchaikovsky (1873).

10. This *Gopak* commences at m.121 in item 4 of *Vakula the Smith* (P.S.S., vol. 35), 121; and at m.78 in item 8 of *Cherevichki* (P.S.S., vol. 39), 124.

11. The whole-tone scale appears in these locations in item 1 of *Vakula the Smith*: mm.431–34; mm.439–42; and mm.447–51 (P.S.S., vol. 35), 76–77. It occurs in these locations in item 2 of *Cherevichki*: mm.177–80; mm.185–88; and mm.193–97 (P.S.S., vol. 39), 61–62.

12. The E flat that appears at the beginning of the Act 3 entr'acte in both *Vakula the Smith* (P.S.S., vol. 35), 205, and in *Cherevichki* (P.S.S., vol. 39), 237, is the pitch around which the succession of chords forms.

13. In the flutes and oboes, Tchaikovsky makes a nod in the direction of this notoriously "incorrect" harmonic—or unharmonic—procedure. They play three successive major seconds, that is, three pairs of adjacent pitches (C sharp-D sharp, E flat-F, F-G) in mm.390–92 of item 1 of *Vakula the Smith* (P.S.S., vol. 35), 351, while the snow swept Chub and Panas are awed by the disappearance of the moon (which the Devil has stolen), and they then transpose that series of sounds a whole tone higher (beginning E flat-F) in mm.400–402. This unorthodox material was excised, along with the rest of the unduly elaborate musical setting of Chub and Panas's escapade, in the revised version of the snowstorm in *Cherevichki*; see note 2, previous.

14. Edward Garden, *Tchaikovsky* (London, 1973, repr.1993), 51.

15. Richard Taruskin, entry on *Cherevichki* in *The New Grove Dictionary of Opera*, ed. Stanley Sadie, vol.1 (London, 1992), 831.

16. Item 15 of *Vakula the Smith* (P.S.S., vol. 35), 256 *et seq.*; and item 21 of *Cherevichki* (P.S.S., vol. 39), 301 *et seq.*

Chapter 5

1. Although Shilovsky's actual contribution to the libretto was slight (see later in the main text), his provision to Tchaikovsky of almost ideal working-conditions—a house mostly to himself on the tranquil Shilovsky estate at Glebovo, near Moscow—must have contributed to the remarkable fluency of inspiration displayed in the music.

2. Chapter 2, stanza 31, lines 13 and 14, in Pushkin's novel.

3. Brown, *Tchaikovsky*, vol. 2, 108.

4. Garden, *Tchaikovsky*, 75.

5. Brown, *Tchaikovsky*, vol. 2, 168.

6. Trans. Galina von Meck, ed. Garden and Gotteri, *"To My Best Friend,"* 187, Tchaikovsky's letter of 1 March 1878.

7. Brown, *Tchaikovsky*, vol. 2, 169.

8. Garden, *Tchaikovsky*, 68.

9. Chapter 3, stanza 32, line 14, in Pushkin's novel.

10. Cf. the observation in chapter 2, concerning *The Voevoda*, about transforming a play into an opera.

11. Brown, *Tchaikovsky*, vol. 2, 195.

12. See chapter 3, stanza 34, in Pushkin's novel.

13. Cf. the remark as translated by R. Taruskin in "'Little Star': An Etude in the Folk Style" in *Musorgsky: In Memoriam 1881–1981*, ed. Malcolm Hamrick Brown (Ann Arbor, 1982), 58.

14. The berry pickers' song, entitled "Song of the Maids," is interpolated between stanzas 39 and 40 in chapter 3.

15. As folk-derived music therefore has, as it were, the last word in that repeated alternation with Western-based music, it causes a sense of propulsive release as a conclusion to Act 1. This is a further instance of Tchaikovsky's suppressive-propulsive technique of composition; cf. note 20, following (and note 10 to chapter 2).

16. The text of *The Singer* has, however, a pastoral flavor, concerning love's sorrow and the distant sound of a pipe in the morning (presumably a shepherd's), which makes it an apt choice for use here, as a portent of the shepherds' music in Act 1 scene 2.

17. Chapter 5, stanza 27, line 9, in Pushkin's novel.

18. Chapter 5, stanza 33, line 9, in Pushkin's novel.

19. In the opera, Tatiana's embarrassment at Triquet's song comes across simply as distaste for being the focus of attention. There is no banquet in the opera.

20. This very effectively continues the use of suppressive-propulsive methods of construction observable in Act 1; cf. note 15, previous (and note 10 to chapter 2).

21. Chapter 8, stanza 48, line 2, in Pushkin's novel.

Chapter 6

1. See H. Zajaczkowski, "Tchaikovsky: The Missing Piece of the Jigsaw Puzzle," *Musical Times* 131 (1990): 238–40. (See also note 5, following.)

2. See *ibid.*, 238, note 6.

3. The name Loré appears in Mermet's *Jeanne d'Arc*, but in relation to the task, undertaken in Tchaikovsky's opera by Dunois, of posing as the king to test the heroine's celestial powers (in Act 2 in both works), which is done by an Ambroise de Loré in the earlier work.

4. Following the premiere in that city were a further four performances, on 30 July, 2 August, 1 October, and 3 October 1882. I am grateful to Professor Jan Smaczny for providing the dates of the Prague performances and the name of the Czech translator.

5. Compare musical examples 1 (Mermet) and 2 (Tchaikovsky) in Zajaczkowski, "Tchaikovsky: The Missing Piece," 239. (See also note 1, previous.)

Chapter 7

1. No. 11 in Balakirev's *Collection of Russian Folksongs* (publ. 1866). Most of the cossack's singing occurs in the immediately preceding number of the opera, item 13, "Folk Scenes" as it is designated in the score, and that number opens with another genuine folk melody, taken from the same collection of Ukrainian folk tunes (no. 110) compiled by Alexander Rubets, from which Tchaikovsky had used material in *Vakula the Smith*. A further three folk songs are employed in *Mazeppa*, including the song of glorification, "Slava," in the entr'acte to Act 3, which Musorgsky had also used in *Boris Godunov*.

2. Abraham, *Slavonic and Romantic Music*, 113 (from the chapter entitled "Tchaïkovsky: Some Centennial Reflections," relating to the centennial, in 1940, of the composer's birth).

3. See Brown, *Tchaikovsky*, vol. 4, *The Final Years (1885–1893)* (London, 1991), the chapter entitled "The Russian Composer: Sixth Symphony," 421 *et seq.*, and the assessment of Tchaikovsky's related suppressive-propulsive methods of composition in the present text (cf. note 10 to chapter 2).

Chapter 8

1. The strings begin playing the second part of the motto-theme in m.14 in the *Manfred* Symphony's first movement.

2. The suppressive-propulsive technique of composition (cf. note 10 to chapter 2) gains particular forcefulness, therefore, by being extended to span most of an opera. This foreshadows the extremely intense use of the technique in Tchaikovsky's last symphony, the *Pathétique* (no. 6), whose entire length it seems to encompass. See Zajaczkowski, *Tchaikovsky's Musical Style*, 45–46.

3. See note 4 to chapter 1.

4. The principle is the same, even though here a genuine folk song is employed, whereas none of the folk-like material in *Eugene Onegin* has been identified as containing any genuine folk themes.

Chapter 9

1. Chapter 5 of Pushkin's short story.

2. In the third chapter of the short story, Pushkin wrote, "'If ever,' said he [Hermann], 'your [the countess's] heart has known the feeling of love,'" etc.

3. See final eighth-note of m.21 to first eighth-note of m.23 in item 2 of the opera: vocal score, P.S.S., vol. 41 (Moscow/Leningrad, 1950), 30–31; the corresponding location in the full score, *ibid.*, vol. 9(a) (Moscow/Leningrad, 1950), 60. (Also, cf. note 14, following.)

4. Liza's only romantic involvement in Pushkin's text, apart from the one-sided one with Hermann, is with her eventual husband, mentioned, as we observed above, in a postscript. However, the name Eletsky (in its feminine form, at any rate: Eletskaia) does receive passing mention in Pushkin's tale, as that of a granddaughter of a Princess Daria Petrovna (see the start of chapter 2).

5. Five pitches of a whole-tone scale, C, D, E, F sharp, and G sharp, occur at the start of these two rapid scalar lines.

6. Cf. the observations in chapter 4 concerning the use of the tritone in the Devil's snowstorm in the opening scene of *Vakula the Smith*.

7. Hermann sings his melody of longing for the unreachable beloved to this rhythm, in common time, beginning with an anacrusis: *eighth-note* (bar line) *4 eighth-notes, dotted quarter-note, eighth-note* (bar line) *2 eighth-notes*.

Tomsky's version of the melody has this more complex and rather cumbersome rhythm, also in common time, but beginning on an anacrusis to the third beat: *eighth-note, half-note* tied (bar line) to a *quarter-note; 2 eighth-notes, quarter-note, 2 eighth-notes* (bar line) *2 quarter-notes*. For the position of these passages in the vocal score, see, respectively, mm.53–55 in item 2, P.S.S., vol. 41, 33–34; and mm.41–43, in item 5, 73. (Also, cf. note 14, following).

8. Comprising E, C, and G sharp.

9. The brief shift to chromatic harmony occurs while Hermann sings, "I'm frightened! The same [taunting] voice. . . ."

10. While Hermann sings, "the old woman!" the clarinets and bassoons suddenly interpolate their presence (m.49 of the scene; see that measure reference in item 16, P.S.S., vol. 9(b) (Moscow/Leningrad, 1950), 189), the sudden darkness of tone-color therefore embodying the very person who is the object of those dark intentions upon which "it is decided" he will act. One notes again his sense of extreme passivity: *he* has not decided; rather, *it is* decided (i.e., Fate determines it so). The prolonged insistence on muted string tone followed by the highly ambivalent dark, yet relief-providing, woodwind phrase is a psychologically potent use of the suppressive-propulsive compositional technique (cf. note 10 to chapter 2, and note 11 to chapter 3), well illustrating that confronting the countess will merely prove to be a false solution to Hermann's problems.

11. Tchaikovsky's treatment here is like a condensation of the actual musical events of the Russian Orthodox burial service. The choral music in that service, setting the words (in Church Slavonic) "I pour out my prayer to the Lord," which is adapted in the opera as well as the verbal text (in modern Russian, beginning "I pray to the Lord"), would not be rendered with a priest intoning against it. The priest does, however, sing a very exhortatory melodic line, including many repetitions of a pitch, elsewhere in the service, which seems to have suggested to Tchaikovsky the manner of Hermann's vocal line as it is actually performed during the choral singing in the opera (cf. note 20, following, and the associated main text).

12. See note 9 to chapter 1.

13. Notated originally as triplet eighth-notes in common time, passing without any change in speed into notation as eighth-notes in twelve-eight time. See the full score of the opera, m.101 *et seq.*, in item 21, P.S.S., vol. 9(c) (Moscow/Leningrad, 1950), 102. (Cf. note 14, following).

14. The theme of longing for the unreachable beloved had included the cello playing a scalar phrase descending from E to G (cf. note 3, previous; these are the same pitches that Hermann had then presently sung). Tomsky's melodic line included a stepwise descent from F sharp to A (regarding the material sung by Hermann and Tomsky, cf. note 7, previous), and the bass clarinet's obsessive reiterations are of a scale descending from C to E (cf. note 13, previous).

15. See m.21 *et seq.*, P.S.S., vol. 41, 8–9.

16. The bass trombone plays the leitmotif as the bass line of a set of three majestic brass chords. Just prior to this, when Chekalinsky had asked Hermann the sum of his

bet, and he had replied "forty thousand," it had played it ruminatively, as a melody. That ruminative quality (the tones rendered softly, but with growing hints of loudness) had formed a highly effective, and ironic, dissociation from the utter madness of the hero's announcement of such a huge bet.

17. Starting in the third beat of m.48 of the opera's finale—see item 24, P.S.S., vol. 9(c), 207—the constantly repeated unit of notes was comprised of a dotted sixteenth-note and a thirty-second-note.

18. From the start of m.66 (*ibid.*, 217) the strings constantly repeat this unit: two triplet sixteenth-notes and a triplet sixteenth-rest.

19. The figuration commencing in the third beat of m.167 (*ibid.*, 240) comprises the simultaneous combination of the following: eighth-notes (played by the horns), triplet eighth-notes (clarinets, bassoon, and cellos), sixteenth-notes (second violins and violas), and triplet sixteenth-notes (first violins), with added instrumentation as the passage proceeds.

20. Unlike the music in that earlier scene, the male chorus has not been identified as being adapted from a liturgical source, and would seem, therefore, to be of Tchaikovsky's own invention. Its general style, however, is clearly based on that of Russian Orthodox chant (cf. note 11, previous, and the associated main text).

Chapter 10

1. The opera is generally known as *Iolanta*, or *Yolanta*, after the eponymous heroine. The playwright Hertz's choice of names—for example, "Jolanthe" for the princess herself—show him rendering French names into Danish spellings. These appear in varying degrees of Russification in the opera (the title character's name looking and sounding quite close to Hertz's version), but in view of the story's setting in Provence (in both play and opera), an attempt has been made in the present text to give all relevant names in a plausibly French form, hence "Yolande." I am grateful for help with matters concerning French from Mrs. Simonne Wheater and Lady Cynthia Morrison-Bell, and for help with those regarding Danish from Mr. Per Troen (in personal communications). See also note 2, following.

2. This name is commonly given as Ebn-Khakia, which reflects the libretto's heavily Russified version of Hertz's Danish spelling, Ebn Jahia, of the common Arabic correlate of the name John: Ibn Yahya. The roots of the name are displayed in the spelling adopted here. The dramaturgic advantage in the distinction (clearly observable in Hertz's play itself) between a group of characters whose names derive from French, and an individual whose name is of Moorish derivation (i.e., Arab–Berber), is of the familiar, set against the potently mysterious unfamiliar, the latter as metaphor of the healing doctor. I am grateful to Dr. Duncan Haldane for help with matters concerning Arabic (in a personal communication). See also note 1, previous.

3. See note 2 to chapter 7.

4. The minuet from the opera *Berenice*, premiered in 1737, by the great German-born composer George Frideric Handel (1685–1759) has been suggested as the source for the imitation here, but that seems very unlikely. Tchaikovsky disliked his music and, more significantly, the overall style of this ensemble has greater stylistic affinities with the second half of the eighteenth century (the Classical period) than its first half (the end of the Baroque period).

SELECTED BIBLIOGRAPHY

The following list represents a very small percentage of the extensive quantity of publications on Tchaikovsky and his work. The main emphasis here is on texts dealing with his operas, and on biographical studies giving the context in the composer's life within which those works were written. Studies of the ballets are also included.

Abraham, G. *On Russian Music* (London, 1939). Includes "*Eugene Onegin* and Tchaikovsky's Marriage," 225.

————. *Slavonic and Romantic Music* (London, 1968). Includes "Tchaikovsky's Operas," 116 (a revision of the chapter entitled "Operas and Incidental Music" in the symposium listed immediately following).

————, ed. *Tchaikovsky: A Symposium* (London, 1945; the American edition appeared the following year, under the title: *The Music of Tchaikovsky*). Includes "Operas and Incidental Music" by G. Abraham, 124 (this is best consulted in revised form in the book listed immediately previous); "The Ballets" by E. Evans, 184.

————. "Tchaikovsky's First Opera [*The Voevoda*]," *Festschrift Karl Gustav Fellerer* (Regensburg, 1962): 12.

Berlin, I. "Tchaikovsky, Pushkin and *Onegin*," *Musical Times* 121 (1980): 163.

Brown, D. *Tchaikovsky: A Biographical and Critical Study*; vol. 1, *The Early Years (1840–1874)* (London, 1978); vol. 2, *The Crisis Years (1874–1878)* (London, 1982); vol. 3, *The Years of Wandering (1878–1885)* (London, 1986); vol. 4, *The Final Years (1885–1893)* (London, 1991). In paperback, the study is reprinted in two parts: vol. 1 (comprising vols. 1 and 2 of the original), *To the Crisis (1840–1878)*, and vol. 2 (vols. 3 and 4 of the original), *The Years of Fame (1878–1893)* (London, 1992).

————. "Tchaikovsky's Marriage," *Musical Times* 123 (1982): 754.

————. "Tchaikovsky's *Mazepa*," *Musical Times* 125 (1984): 696.

Garden, E. *Tchaikovsky* (London, 1973).

John, N., ed. *Eugene Onegin* (London, 1988).

Kearney, L., ed. *Tchaikovsky and His World* (Princeton, 1998). This symposium includes "Tchaikovsky's Tatiana [heroine of *Eugene Onegin*]" by C. Emerson, 216; "On the Role of Gremin: Tchaikovsky's *Eugene Onegin*" by K. Grönke (trans. A. D. Humel), 220; "Review of *The Maid of Orleans* [1899]" by N. Kashkin (trans. M. Kostalevsky, notes and commentary by L. Kearney), 234; "Tchaikovsky Androgyne: *The Maid of Orleans*" by L. Kearney, 239; "Tchaikovsky and the Russian 'Silver Age [the period from the 1890s to the Russian Civil War]'" by A. Klimovitsky (trans. A. D. Humel), which includes important observations on *The Queen of Spades* and *Iolanta* [*Yolande*], 319. The texts by Grönke and Klimovitsky were originally published in German in the journal listed immediately following (ed. Kohlhase).

Kohlhase, T., ed. *Čajkovskij-Studien* [*Tchaikovsky Studies*; journal of the Tchaikovsky Society in Klin, Russia, and Tübingen, Germany; the composer's name in the journal is spelled according to the International Organization for Standardization's transliteration system], 1 (1995). Published form of papers read at the 1993 symposium in Tübingen to commemorate the centennial of Tchaikovsky's death. Includes "Zur Rolle des Gremin in Čajkovskijs Oper *Evgenij Onegin*" by K. Grönke, 127; "Čajkovskij und das russische 'Silberne Zeitalter'" by A. Klimovitsky, 155; Čajkovskij und die literarische Kultur Russlands" by R.-D. Kluge, 165; "Čajkovskijs *Pikovaja Dama* [*The Queen of Spades*] und die Tradition der französischen Opéra-comique-Ballade" by L. Lauer, 199; "Čajkovskij mit den Augen Stravinskijs gesehen: Zum Verhältnis von ontologischer und psychisch determinierter Zeit in den Opern Čajkovskijs" by S. Neef, 223; "Modest Čajkovskij: In His Brother's Shadow" by A. Poznansky, which includes important observations on the composer and his brother's operatic collaborations, 233; "On Čajkovskij's Psychopathology and Its Relationship with His Creativity" by H. Zajaczkowski (a revised and expanded version of "Tchaikovsky: The Missing Piece of the Jigsaw Puzzle," *Musical Times* 131 (1990): 238), which addresses *The Maid of Orléans*, 307. The texts by Grönke and Klimovitsky were reprinted in English translation in the book listed immediately previous (ed. Kearney).

Lloyd-Jones, D. "A Background to *Iolanta*," *Musical Times* 109 (1968): 225.

von Meck, G., trans. *"To My Best Friend"*: *Correspondence between Tchaikovsky and Nadezhda von Meck 1876–1878*. Edited by E. Garden and N. Gotteri (Oxford, 1993). The translator was the composer's great-niece and his patroness's granddaughter.

Mihailovic, A., ed. *Tchaikovsky and His Contemporaries: A Centennial Symposium* (Westport, 1999). Published form of papers read at the 1993 conference at Hofstra University to commemorate the centennial of Tchaikovsky's death. Includes "Culture and Nationalism: Tchaikovsky's Visions of Russia in *The Oprichnik*" by S. B. Eggers, 139; "The Intrigue of Love and Illusion in Tchaikovsky's *The Oprichnik*" by A. Swartz, 147; "Tchaikovsky's *Eugene Onegin*: Tatiana and Lensky, the Third Couple" by T. Bullard, 157; "'But Was My Eugene Happy?': Musical and Dramatic Tensions in *Eugene Onegin*" by B. Nelson, 167; "Musical Historicism in *The Queen Of Spades*" by J. Parakilas, 177.

Orlova, A. *Tchaikovsky: A Self-Portrait* (Oxford, 1990).

Poznansky, A. *Tchaikovsky: The Quest for the Inner Man* (New York, 1991).

———, and B. Langston (compilers). *The Tchaikovsky Handbook: A Guide to the Man and His Music (Russian Music Studies*, founding ed. M. Brown), vol. 1, *Thematic Catalogue of Works, Catalogue of Photographs, Autobiography*, vol. 2, *Catalogue of Letters, Genealogy, Bibliography* (Bloomington/Indianapolis, 2002).

Seibert, D. "The Dramaturgy of Tchaikovsky's *Mazeppa*: An Interview with [the conductor of the English National Opera's production of that work] Mark Elder," *Music Review* 49 (1988): 275.

Sylvester, R. *Tchaikovsky's Complete Songs: A Companion with Texts and Translations* (Bloomington/Indianapolis, 2002).

Taruskin, R. *Defining Russia Musically: Historical and Hermeneutical Essays* (Princeton, 1997). Includes various important observations on Tchaikovsky's operas, particularly *Eugene Onegin* in "P. I. Chaikovsky [Tchaikovsky] and the Ghetto," 48, and a valuable study, "Chaikovsky and the Human: A Centennial Essay," 239, commencing with an assessment of George Eliot's *Mr. Gilfil's Love-Story* (from *Scenes of Clerical Life*) as a possible source of the composer's next opera on the verge of his untimely death.

Taylor, P. *Gogolian Interludes: Gogol's Story "Christmas Eve" as the Subject of the Operas by Tchaikovsky [Cherevichki] and Rimsky-Korsakov [Christmas Eve]* (London and Wellingborough, 1984). Contains translations not only of both libretti, but also of Gogol's original story.

———. *The Oprichnik: Translation and Notes* (London and Wellingborough, 1980). Contains a translation of the libretto.

Warrack, J. *Tchaikovsky* (London, 1973).

———. *Tchaikovsky Ballet Music* (London, 1979).

Wiley, R. *Tchaikovsky's Ballets* (Oxford, 1985).

———. "The Symphonic Element in [the ballet] *Nutcracker*," *Musical Times* 125 (1984): 693.

Zajaczkowski, H. *Russian Music Studies*. Vol. 19, *Tchaikovsky's Musical Style*, edited by M. Brown (Ann Arbor/London, 1987).

INDEX

The use of n *indicates a note on the page.*

Ministry of Justice (St. Petersburg), 105, 106
Minkus, Ludwig, ix
Mozart, Wolfgang, 47, 109
Musorgsky, Modest, 3, 11, 28, 29, 30, 107
Napoleon Bonaparte, 109
Nápravník, Eduard, 15, 26, 46, 76, 99
Novotny, V., 46

Odoevsky, Vladimir, Prince, 4
Opéra, The (Paris theater), 15
Ostrovsky, Alexander, 7, 9, 10, 17, 106

Padilla y Ramos, Mariano, 106
Palchikova, Maria, 105
Panaev Theater (St. Petersburg), 16
Pavlovna, Elena, Grand Duchess, 23
Perrault, Charles, 110
Peter I (the Great), Tsar
  as historical character, 2, 49
  as operatic figure, 49, 50, 51, 53, 55
Petrova, Anastasia, 105
Piccioli, Luigi, 105
Polonsky, Iakov, 23
Poznansky, Alexander, x
Prokofiev, Sergei, ix, 108, 109
Pushkin, Alexander, x, xi, 2, 4–5, 31, 33–40, 42, 49, 52, 71, 76–78, 110

Rachinsky, Sergei, 12
Rakhmaninov, Sergei, 108
Rimsky-Korsakov, Nikolai, 3, 5, 6, 9, 28, 29, 30, 107
Ristori, Giovanni, 3
Rossini, Gioachino, 4, 18
Rubets, Alexander, 28–29
Rubinstein, Anton, 106
Rubinstein, Nikolai, 33, 106, 109

Russian Musical Society (St. Petersburg), 23, 106
Russian Register, The, 34, 107

von Schiller, Friedrich, 43, 47
School of Jurisprudence (St. Petersburg), 105
Scribe, Eugène, 15, 18
Serov, Alexander, 13, 23, 53
Shakespeare, William, 37, 52, 106, 107, 110
Shilovsky, Konstantin, 31, 39
Shostakovich, Dmitry, 108
Shpazhinsky, Ippolit, 59, 64, 65
Solovëv, Nikolai, 71
Spinoza, Baruch, 19
Stasov, Vladimir, 107, 109
State Tchaikovsky House-Museum (Klin, Russia), xi
Stravinsky, Igor, ix
Sumarokov, Alexander, 3
Susanin, Ivan, as historical character, 4. *For Susanin as operatic figure see* Glinka, Mikhail, *Life for the Tsar, A*, aria "They guess the truth"
Synod, Russian, 106

Taneyev, Sergei, 34
Taruskin, Richard, 18, 30, 52, 53
Tchaikovskaia, Alexandra (composer's mother, *née* Assier), 105
Tchaikovskaia, Alexandra (composer's sister), 105
Tchaikovskaia, Zinaida (composer's half-sister), 105
Tchaikovsky, Anatoly (composer's brother), 105
Tchaikovsky, Ilia (composer's father), 105, 109
Tchaikovsky, Ippolit (composer's brother), 105

orchestral depiction of blindness,
99, 100, 101, 102
orchestral depiction of madness,
55–56, 89–92, 94, 100
oriental idiom, use of, 5
operas
  Cherevichki (revision of *Vakula
    the Smith*), 1, 23–28, 30, 109,
    110
  Chorus of Flowers and Insects
    (fragment of abortive
    Mandragora), 12
  Enchantress, The, ix, 2, 59–70,
    100, 110
  Eugene Onegin, ix, x, xi, 2, 3, 8,
    19, 27, 30, 31–42, 46, 48, 52,
    54, 64, 66, 70, 79, 96, 103,
    108, 109
  Maid of Orléans, The, ix, 2, 19,
    26, 43–48, 52, 53, 54, 66,
    100, 103, 108, 109
  Mazeppa, xi, 1–2, 10, 49–57, 59,
    64, 66, 67, 89, 96, 100, 109
  Oprichnik, The, 1–2, 11, 12,
    13–22, 29, 30, 33, 35, 46, 47,
    52, 53, 54, 65–66, 67, 107
  Queen of Spades, The, ix, x, xi, 2,
    3, 30, 71–96, 100, 103, 110
  Undine, 1, 12, 106, 107
  Vakula the Smith, 8, 23, 26–30,
    33, 103, 107, 108, 109
  Voevoda, The, 1, 7–12, 13,
    16–17, 18, 33, 52, 100, 106,
    107
  Yolande, 1, 5, 97–104, 110
orchestral music, miscellaneous
  Characteristic Dances, 116n5
  Serenade in C major for Strings,
    109
orchestral suites
  no. 1 in D minor, 108, 109
  no. 2 in C major, 109
  no. 3 in G major, 109

  no. 4 (*Mozartiana*) in G major,
    109
orchestral works in one
    movement
  1812 (festival overture), 109
  Fatum ("Fate," symphonic
    poem), 106
  Francesca da Rimini (symphonic
    fantasia), 34, 69, 108
  Hamlet (fantasy-overture),
    110
  Romeo and Juliet (fantasy-
    overture), 52, 106, 107, 109
  Storm, The (overture), 106
  Tempest, The (symphonic
    fantasia), 107
  Voevoda, The (symphonic
    ballad), 110
as pedagogical author, 106
piano music
  Anastasie Valse, 105
relationship to the Mighty
    Handful, 106–107
religious music
  Liturgy of St. John
    Chrysostom, 108
  Vesper Service, 109
remote chords joined pivotally,
    use of, 21, 29, 79, 83, 87
as reviewer, 34, 106, 107
revival of his operas in late
    twentieth century, 2–3,
    115n2, 117n1
Russian folk and Western art-
    music styles, synthesis of,
    9–10, 54
Russian folk-influence, use of, 4,
    8, 9, 18, 31, 32, 33, 35, 36,
    37–38, 47, 52, 60, 64, 65,
    66–67, 72, 75, 107, 108
Russian folk songs, use of, 8, 9,
    13, 14, 26, 35, 51, 52, 53, 59,
    64, 70

ABOUT THE AUTHOR

HENRY ZAJACZKOWSKI is the author of *Tchaikovsky's Musical Style* and a contributor to *Music Review, Musical Times,* and the journal of the Tchaikowsky-Gesellschaft. He has lectured about music on BBC Radio and at Lincoln Center in New York City. He teaches music privately in London.